T0214907

Industrial System Engineering for Drones

A Guide with Best Practices for Designing

Neeraj Kumar Singh
Porselvan Muthukrishnan
Satyanarayana Sanpini

Apress®

Industrial System Engineering for Drones: A Guide with Best Practices for Designing

Neeraj Kumar Singh
Bangalore, India

Porselvan Muthukrishnan
Bangalore, India

Satyanarayana Sanpini
Bangalore, India

ISBN-13 (pbk): 978-1-4842-3533-1
https://doi.org/10.1007/978-1-4842-3534-8

ISBN-13 (electronic): 978-1-4842-3534-8

Managing Director, Apress Media LLC: Welmoed Spahr
Acquisitions Editor: Natalie Pao
Development Editor: James Markham
Coordinating Editor: Jessica Vakili

Cover image designed by Freepik (www.freepik.com)

Distributed to the book trade worldwide by Springer Science+Business Media New York, 233 Spring Street, 6th Floor, New York, NY 10013. Phone 1-800-SPRINGER, fax (201) 348-4505, e-mail orders-ny@springer-sbm.com, or visit www.springeronline.com. Apress Media, LLC is a California LLC and the sole member (owner) is Springer Science + Business Media Finance Inc (SSBM Finance Inc). SSBM Finance Inc is a **Delaware** corporation.

For information on translations, please e-mail rights@apress.com, or visit www.apress.com/rights-permissions.

Apress titles may be purchased in bulk for academic, corporate, or promotional use. eBook versions and licenses are also available for most titles. For more information, reference our Print and eBook Bulk Sales web page at www.apress.com/bulk-sales.

Any source code or other supplementary material referenced by the author in this book is available to readers on GitHub via the book's product page, located at www.apress.com/978-1-4842-3533-1. For more detailed information, please visit www.apress.com/source-code.

Printed on acid-free paper

Dedicated to my sons, Anant and Atulya,
for filling my life with joy and inspiration

—Neeraj

Dedicated to my teachers and mentors

—Satya

Dedicated to my teachers and mentors

—Porselvan

Table of Contents

About the Authors

Neeraj Kumar Singh has been a Platform Architect for Intel Client platforms for more than 12 years. His areas of expertise are hardware/software co-design, SoC system/platform architecture, and system software design and development. Neeraj is the author of *System on Chip Interfaces for Low Power Design* and *The Impact of Loop Unrolling on Controller Delay in High Level Synthesis*.

Porselvan Muthukrishnan has been a Hardware/System Design Engineer for Intel IOT platforms for over 10 years. His area of expertise is hardware/system design. Porselvan is currently working on system designs for connected home, connected cars, and other IoT devices.

Satyanarayana Sanpini has been working in the fields of low-power embedded systems architecture, SoC definition, architecture, and design for the past 17+ years. He has contributed in various technical positions at start-ups Ittiam, Beceem Communications, and MNCs Broadcom, and also Qualcomm and Intel. He is currently based out of Bangalore, India and works at Intel India Center. Satya obtained his M.Tech degree in Electronics Design from Indian Institute of Science (IISc), Bangalore, India. Apart from a passion for technology, Satya likes to spend time with his young kids and explore nature's grandeur through travel and trek.

Acknowledgements

We would like to express gratitude to the people who helped us through this book; some of them directly and many others indirectly.

It's impossible to not risk missing someone, but we will attempt anyway.

First and foremost, we would like to acknowledge Vinay K C and Balachandar Santhanam for their guidance and time in review. Vinay and Bala, your detailed review helped the book significantly in terms of structure, content, and quality; thank you very much!!

We would like to thank Intel management for the support and encouragement.

Above all, we thank our families and friends for their understanding, support, and being continuous source of encouragement.

CHAPTER 1

Introduction

System design is a discipline of creating a system/product, starting from requirements to the final deployment in the field. It is a very vast subject and encompasses multiple cross-functional domains such as market research, planning, product definition, hardware design, software design, industrial design, validation, certification, etc. It is very difficult to cover all of these aspects in detail in a single book. This may be why few references cover the system design in detail. This book is an attempt to provide a brief introduction to the system design discipline.

As anyone can understand, a vast variety of systems are possible in the real world. The focus of this book is a typical electromechanical system design, with emphasis on electrical hardware system design concepts. You will be taken through the processes and methodologies comprehensively using the fairly complex electromechanical system of a drone as an example. While this book primarily focuses on the electrical part of the system design, other critical disciplines like mechanicals and software are covered at a high level to give a complete perspective of the system design. To give you a feel of designing a system from scratch yourself, at many places the content is presented from a first-person perspective. By end of the book, you will get a glimpse of how multiple subsystems are developed or chosen carefully (components are either "make" or "buy") to get a flawless system (through the drone example). The focus areas vary dynamically, but "make" components are emphasized more than "buy" components. Hardware is always a make item for most of the system design, so that's why it's covered in so much detail.

© Neeraj Kumar Singh, Porselvan Muthukrishnan, Satyanarayana Sanpini 2019
N. K. Singh et al., *Industrial System Engineering for Drones*,
https://doi.org/10.1007/978-1-4842-3534-8_1

The organization of the book is as follows. In Chapter 1, we start with brief description of the drone system and its critical components. In Chapter 2, the typical system design flow details are presented. Chapter 3 delves into the drone system's key ingredients and selection procedure. In Chapter 4, the electronic hardware development process is covered in detail. Chapter 5 covers typical procedures and checks followed as part of a system bring-up. In Chapter 6, the software processes and real-time software that go into drone-like systems are discussed. Chapter 7 concludes the book with coverage of the final certification processes a system needs to go through before deployment. Two appendixes provide additional basics and references.

What Is a Drone?

An unmanned aerial vehicle (UAV), commonly known as a drone, is an aircraft without a human pilot onboard. UAVs are a component of an unmanned aircraft system, which includes a UAV, a ground-based controller, and a system of communications between the two. The flight of UAVs may operate with various degrees of autonomy, either under remote control by a human operator or autonomously by onboard computers.

Drones are classified into different categories based on the applications. Applications are broad, and from the design perspective, generally fall under three major groups: military, industrial (`enterprise`), and commercial.

Military

Drones in military applications are used for anti-aircraft target practice, intelligence gathering and, more controversially, as weapons platforms.

Industrial

The integration of drones and IoT (Internet of Things) technology has created numerous industrial and enterprise use cases: drones working with on-ground IOT sensor networks can help agricultural companies monitor land and crops, energy companies survey power lines and operational equipment, and insurance companies monitor properties for claims and/or policies.

Commercial

The commercial field is a growing development, where the largest, strongest, fastest, and most capable drones on the market are targeted toward the professional community. They are the types of machines that the movie industry puts to work and that commercial agencies use to inspect infrastructure. Some impressive self-piloted drones survey individual farmer's fields. Commercial drones are the smaller consumer products that make up just a tiny portion of the overall drone market. Figure 1-1 shows the form factor of a commercial drone.

Figure 1-1. Commercial drone

Parts of a Drone System

From an engineer's view, the key parts of a drone system are the hardware, software, and mechanical elements; and a perfect balance between the three provides a flawless system design.

Hardware

Hardware is the electrical part of the drone system, which is eventually a PCBA (`printed circuit board assembly`). Hardware is a multilayer PCB that accommodates the SOC (`system on a chip`) and different components of the subsystems interconnected through copper traces (part of the PCB) or physical wires. Figure 1-2 shows the PCBA assembled with SOC and subsystems on the top side (`primary side`).

Figure 1-2. *PCBA mounted with SOC and subsystems*

The SOC

The SOC is a miniature computer on a chip of a present generation systems, especially a drone system. It's a semiconductor device and an integrated circuit that usually integrates digital, analog, mixed signal, and radio frequency devices on a single chip. SOCs are most commonly used in mobile computing and embedded systems.

In general, there are three distinguishable types of SOCs: SOCs built around a microcontroller, SOCs built around a microprocessor, and specialized SOCs designed for specific applications that do not fit into the above two categories.

SOC usually consume less power and have a lower cost than the multichip systems they replace.

Note   Intel Core, Atom, and Quark processors are SOCs on a single package.

Figure 1-3 shows a typical SOC that integrate digital, analog, and mixed signal devices on a single chip. The device at the center of the SOC is the silicon, and some capacitors are distributed on the top side of the SOC. The bottom side of the SOC shows pins (called as balls in a ball grid array), which are soldered on to a PCB to establish the connection with the subsystems through PCB traces. You'll see more details on this in later sections.

Figure 1-3. *Top and bottom views of the SOC*

Subsystems

Subsystems or electrical subsystems are technologies required in a system to fulfill the intended usage of the system.

Broadly speaking, subsystems fall into any one of the following computer architecture parts: input, output, storage, and communication devices.

Input

A touch panel, keyboard, mouse, microphone, camera, sensors, and remote control are some examples of input devices of a system.

Output

Displays, speakers, motors, fans, and LEDs are some examples of output devices of a system.

Storage

Memory, flash, hard disk drive, optical drive, secure digital, and solid state drive are some examples of the storage devices of a system.

Communication Devices

Wired LAN (local area network), wireless LAN, mobile networks (3G, 4G, and LTE), GPS (Global Positioning System), and USB are some examples of the communication devices of a systems.

All of the subsystems listed above may or may not be a part of a particular drone design. The target application picks the right subsystems to be part of the drone system design.

For example, if the intended application of a drone is surveillance, it should be equipped with a high resolution camera and the SOC used in the system should be capable of accepting and processing the high speed data from that camera. The PCBA should be designed in such a way as to interconnect the high speed data between SOC and the camera module and then be capable of transmitting the live or recorded data via the wireless communication modules.

Besides SOC, the camera module, wireless module (WiFi/3G/4G modules), memory, internal storage, sensors, and flight controllers are the basic required subsystems for a surveillance drone. Figure 1-4 is the transparent view of the internal parts of the drone, highlighting a few high-level subsystems, which are visible.

Figure 1-4. *Parts of a drone*

Subsystems play an important role in defining the specifications of the product. ("Product" is the right term for a system when in production stage and available in the market). An end user will see these subsystems as a feature list when selecting a product. A typical drone will have the features listed in Table 1-1.

Table 1-1. *Basic Features of a Drone*

Features	Specifications
Camera pixels	2MP, 720PHD
Controller	2.4GHz
Channels	4 channels
Gyroscope	6-axis control
Distance	Control by phone about 164ft/
	Control by controller about 262ft
Battery for quadcopter	3.7V 900mAh li-po battery

Table 1-2 lists the specifications covering additional internal features of the drone system. It must again be noted that the specification here is for an example drone and will vary from one drone system to another. As seen earlier, some subsystems from the list may or may not be required for the target application of the system.

Table 1-2. *Detailed Features of a Drone System*

Subsystems	Features	Specifications
NETWORK	Technology	GSM / CDMA / HSPA / EVDO / LTE
PROCESSING	CPU	Quad-core 2.34 GHz
	GPU	6-core graphics
MEMORY	Card slot	No
	Internal	32/128/256 GB, 2 GB RAM
CAMERA	Primary	12 MP (f/1.8, 28mm, 1/3"), phase detection autofocus, OIS, quad-LED dual-tone flash, check quality
	Features	Geo-tagging, simultaneous 4K video and 8MP image recording, touch focus, face/smile detection, HDR (photo/panorama)
	Video	2160p@30fps, 1080p@30/60/120fps, 720p@240fps, check quality
	Secondary	7 MP (f/2.2, 32mm), 1080p@30fps, 720p@240fps, face detection, HDR, panorama
AUDIO	Alert types	Vibration
	Loudspeaker	Yes, with stereo speakers
	3.5mm jack	No

(continued)

Table 1-2. (*continued*)

Subsystems	Features	Specifications
COMMS	WLAN	Wi-Fi 802.11 a/b/g/n/ac, dual-band, hotspot
	Bluetooth	4.2, A2DP, LE
	GPS	Yes, with A-GPS, GLONASS, GALILEO, QZSS
	NFC	Yes
	USB	2.0, proprietary reversible connector
SENSORS	Sensors	Fingerprint, accelerometer, gyro, proximity, compass, barometer

Software

There are three or maybe four categories of software that we'd use on the drone system:

1. *Firmware components*: Many of the HW components (devices) that we put on a system today are not just passive hardware components; they have associated firmware that can help offload certain activities without requiring the CPU's attention.

2. *OS and drivers*: Typically, in an OS-based environment, to maintain the coherency of device usage and establish a level of security, the SW is divided into system and application domains. Different OSes use different terminologies for the same: system and application domains. This separation typically uses the protection and separation mechanism provided by hardware. And different SOC architectures implement and/or

provide different ways for protection and separation. Broadly speaking, there are two parts to the system part of the software:

a. The controllers' and devices' drivers, which provide access to the hardware and serialize the access requests from different SW components.

b. The other part is the overall management of resources (devices/controllers, processor, and memory), and scheduling, etc. It also provides infrastructure for communication across various beings (hardware and software) on the system. This part is commonly referred as the operating system (OS). Given the nature of the usages, drones need to use a real-time operating system (RTOS). RTOS is a category of operating systems that provide a mechanism to guarantee higher bound to a process completion.

3. *Sensing, navigation, and control*: With drones being UAVs, sensing, navigation, and control are of the utmost importance. The first piece of this crucial part is the sensing infrastructure, which feeds the navigation system, which triggers control decisions.

4. *Application-specific components*: In addition to the first three fundamental components, there are likely to be some application-specific components (both software and hardware). For illustration, taking the example of the surveillance drone, there will be image capture, processing, and transmit-related components on the system. The application-specific components make use of the "OS and driver" piece in order to accomplish the goal.

Figure 1-5 shows the logical view of the software components of a typical drone system, as just discussed.

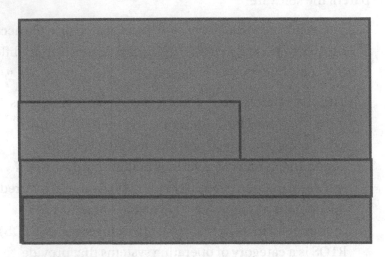

Figure 1-5. *Logical view of the drone software stack*

Mechanical

The mechanical system is basically the enclosures, form factor, or simple ID (industrial design) of the drone. The ID determines the exterior and appearance of the drone. The ID of the drone will usually have numerous mechanical parts in a complicated assembly with electrical parts interconnected through mechanical or thermal interconnects.

The most popular drone, seen in Figure 1-1, has a quadcopter built from an X-frame or H-frame with four servo motor/propeller units on each end with numerous other mechanical parts along with the PCBA enclosed in plastic.

A drone with frame as a base includes propellers, motors, landing gear, body (usually PCBA, flight controllers, and motor drivers), and a battery.

Note   Heavier drones are powered using alternate fuels other than batteries, such as solar power or gasoline. Drones operating with these fuels are not only heavy but they use different technology and are designed for different purposes.

The PCBA is usually considered a single mechanical part of a system. The PCBA is the energy consuming part of the system and dissipates heat while doing the operation, so it needs a cooling system.

A typical electronics hardware setup will have a heatsink to spread the heat generated by the integrated circuits, which is often accompanied by a fan on the head to blow out the excess heat. The fan needs separate, additional power on top of the system power and this kind of cooling is termed as "active cooling," whereas heatsink-based cooling without a fan is called as "passive cooling." Passive cooling doesn't need any extra power.

For a very low-power system, the ground layers of the PCBA spread the heat and become self-sustaining without any extra cooling system/ mechanism. Figure 1-6 shows the discrete mechanical parts of an ID excluding enclosures. Most mechanical parts are customized for the design, which can be designed in-house or can be created using third-party mechanical expertise designers. Some mechanical parts like motors, screws, and cables will be available off the shelf and can be purchased directly from third-party vendors.

Figure 1-6. *Mechanical parts of a drone*

Ground-Based Controllers and Accessories

Ground-based controllers and accessories are essential items required for a drone to operate, just like any other electronic gadget available on the market.

The most important accessory is the RF-based remote controller for the drone, which helps to control the UAV from a remote location. Alternatively, the drones can also be controlled through a smartphone, thanks to the latest advancement in the technologies, but only if the drones are capable of connecting to the 3G/LTE mobile network.

Other functions like video streaming and capture can be done through a smartphone application or GUI (`graphics user interface`) from a host controller.

The majority of the drones today are battery operated; a charger/power adapter is the other most important accessory of the system.

Other optional accessories are the USB data cable and docking station. Figure 1-7 shows the typical accessories of the commercial drone, if the system design supports them.

Figure 1-7. *Typical accessories for a drone*

Summary

The intent of the book is to cover the basics of system design with the primary focus on the electrical hardware system design. A drone system will be used as an example to drive the concepts.

A drone is a complex electromechanical system with multiple discrete components connected directly or indirectly. Critical subsystems of a drone are presented as a starting point. Further details of many subsystem designs will be covered in the following chapters.

CHAPTER 2

Drone System Design Flow

In the previous chapter, you learned about the fundamentals of a drone system and the integral parts of a drone, which are basically hardware, software, and mechanicals. You also learned about the subsystems of the drone and how they map to the features of the drone as a product.

In this chapter, we will primarily discuss the flow of drone system design. The flow will assist you in the deep learning of the system and its applications. Design flow starts with the architecture, which includes all the system elements or blocks, which we will describe in detail in each section on hardware, software, and mechanicals for a quick understanding of the cross-functional engineers and any other team that contributes to the system design.

In this chapter, we'll focus on the general flow of the system design with annotations relating to the drone system design. We'll also define, at a high level, what example design we will take for illustration purposes. The details on various stages or steps relating to the specific drone system design will be covered in the upcoming chapters.

System Design

System design, in general, is usually done by a group of experts (or team) involving expertise from hardware, software, and mechanical engineers

© Neeraj Kumar Singh, Porselvan Muthukrishnan, Satyanarayana Sanpini 2019
N. K. Singh et al., *Industrial System Engineering for Drones*,
https://doi.org/10.1007/978-1-4842-3534-8_2

with different and complementary skill sets. This group of people typically consists of component engineers, CAD engineers, design engineers, test engineers, and program managers. Many times the composition of the team depends upon the nature of the product being designed and developed.

In general, the product design process typically involves three main aspects: specification, architecture, and implementation.

Requirement Specification

Requirement specification is the first step in any system design. The requirement specification step involves gathering the requirements and converting them into detailed document collaterals which act as the starting point for various teams involved in the design. For a complicated electromechanical system like a drone, multiple documents from electrical, mechanical, and software are required to understand the design.

A single source document, which is accountable to generate all of the other architectural documents in sequence or parallel, is the product requirement document (PRD).

The PRD is the scope of the target system, created with input from the marketing team based on the extensive market research, contributions from the customer, and input from the engineering team. The engineering team works in parallel to gather the requirements and collating the reports and results from feasibility analysis. The PRD can sometimes be interchanged with the system requirement document (SRD). While different organizations use different terminology, generally PRD is the terminology used by the marketing team, external teams, or non-engineering teams, whereas the term SRD is used by the design team or engineering team.

Architecture

The engineering team generates the engineering specification in response to the PRD, which addresses the possibility of fulfilling the requirements of the PRD or a deviation or alternate way of fulfilling the requirements. There are several other design documents that represent the hardware, software, and mechanicals at a high level to explain the sections to external, cross-functional, and customer teams to keep everybody on the same page before starting the actual design.

Mechanical Design

The mechanical concept is usually done in a CAD (computer-aided design) tool. The output is usually a standard file format that can be opened/imported in any CAD application software or multiple image files showing the sectional view such as top, bottom, and cross-sectional view of the target 3D model concept. Figure 2-1 shows the partially completed or work-in-progress 3D model file developed using CAD tools of an X-frame of a drone. This is not limited to the X-frame; other mechanical parts like enclosures, screws, and propellers need to be designed in the same way to complete the 3D model. The electrical components like the PCB and the interconnects are modeled in a different electrical CAD tool and are imported into a mechanical CAD tool to get the complete 3D concept of the drone. The dimensions and tolerances of the parts need to be more accurate for the 3D model in order to avoid any defect during manufacturing. The mechanical concept is usually a part of the engineering specification and it presents the opportunities and risks of meeting the requirements from the PRD.

Although the perfect balance between hardware, software, and mechanical ingredients is required for an outstanding system design, one of the key selling points for a consumer drone is the aesthetics of the mechanical enclosures. Therefore, a lot of focus is on the mechanical design in the initial phase. Mechanical design, like most other design work, is an iterative process; that means you start with an initial concept and then iterate over it based on feedback. Hardware and software go through the minor changes in the middle or later point of time during the detailed design phase.

There are different mechanical CAD tools available to develop the 3D models. Output files are generated in a specific format to easily view using other applications or viewers. Viewers are the light version of the same or different CAD tool, and don't require any license and can be installed on any hardware with minimum graphics. Usually viewers are used by cross-functional engineers to view the actual 3D model of the product during the architecture and design phase. One such example is shown in Figure 2-1. A completed X-frame step file is viewed using step viewer tool. A step file is the most widely used file format (.STEP). An ISO 10303 standard format can represent 3D objects in CAD and related information.

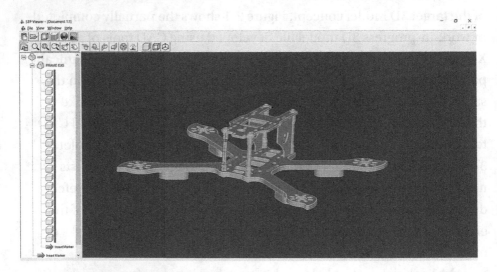

Figure 2-1. *A 3D model of the X-frame*

The mechanical design process has evolved over last few years with the rise of 3D printing. New consumer-friendly 3D printers can produce dimensional objects. The 3D printers print (`create`) objects with a plastic-like substance as opposed to traditional printers that spread ink across a page. Building a prototype from the 3D mechanical model is cooler these days, unlike hardware design, which still stay as a longer pole in the system design.

Hardware Design

In the past, new product design and development in the field of electronics was by definition hardware design. Today, this isn't the case; it is only a part of the equation. Hardware design at a concept level or an architectural level is usually explained with an electrical block diagram with all the electrical ingredients interconnected through the compatible electrical interfaces. Generally, all the ingredients are connected to the SOC, which is often considered the brain of the system. A few ingredients can connect to each other directly rather connecting to SOC if the ingredients are independent or the functionality of the specific ingredient demands. The key list of ingredients required for the system also explains the product structure at a high level. Figure 2-2 shows the hardware block diagram, which includes part numbers of the devices used and also completes the key bill of materials of the hardware. These are the minimum required hardware blocks to build a drone; more details in the upcoming chapters.

The hardware of the system is nothing but a PCBA. This block diagram completely transforms into a PCBA, which is discussed in more detail in the implementation part of this book.

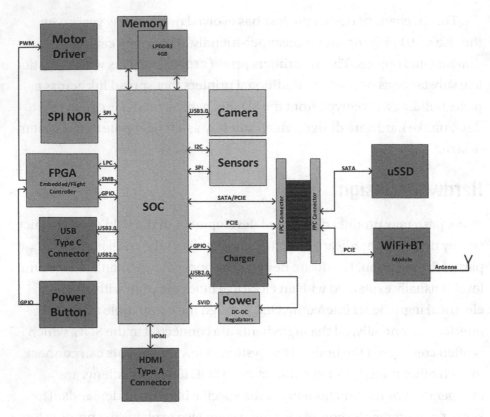

Figure 2-2. *Drone hardware block diagram and key BOM*

Software Design

In a system, the complete functionality is co-provided by hardware (HW) and software (SW). Based on the product PRD, HW and SW partitioning is done. In other words, it shows what part of the functionality is provided by chosen HW blocks and what is covered in SW. After the partition is made, the SW design and development can start straightaway. There are SW design practices and a SW development life cycle that is followed. The focus of this book is not the software design flow since it's very well established and enough references are available relating to SW product life cycle.

Implementation

This is where the designers narrow their ideas, which can be guaranteed successes, and from there they can outline their plan to make the product. In this phase, the engineers implement the design and build the prototype as per the plan outlined in the previous step. The last stage of this phase is when the product is tested, and from there, improvements are made. The implementation part is explained in detail in upcoming chapters of this book.

Specifications for Our Drone, "Crop Squad"

For the illustration and discussion in this book, we are going to take the below specification for the design throughout this book. The specification given in Table 2-1 also corresponds to the architecture diagram given in Figure 2-2.

Table 2-1. *Drone Hardware Specifications*

Subsystems	Features	Specifications
PROCESSING	CPU	Quad-core 2.34 GHz
MEMORY	RAM	4 GB
	External	SD Card 128 GB
	Internal	uSSD 128 GB
CAMERA	Hyperspectral imaging	Line scan, 600-975nm, >100 bands Interface: USB 3.1
AUDIO	Alert types	Beep, vibration
	Loudspeaker	Yes, with stereo speakers(need basis)

(continued)

Table 2-1. (*continued*)

Subsystems	Features	Specifications
COMMS	WLAN	Wi-Fi 802.11 a/b/g/n/ac, dual-band,
	Bluetooth	4.2, A2DP, LE
	GPS	Yes, with A-GPS, GLONASS, GALILEO, QZSS
DISPLAY	HDMI	Yes
IO	Type C	Type C USB3.1 for data communication, charging
SENSORS	Sensors	Accelerometer, gyro, proximity, compass, barometer
OTHERS	FPGA	Flight controllers, embedded controllers, motor PWM controllers

Mechanical Design

As mentioned in the previous section, defining (`creating`) or choosing the right mechanical design of the system is the starting point. In the following sections, we will talk about the key aspects of making mechanical design choices.

A drone is not an entirely new concept. The term was used in the early 1900s for UAVs. Different types of drones are already in use for various purposes. Keeping that as a base and the target application in mind, a perfect mechanical design needs to be created that, along with hardware and software, must fulfill all the requirements listed in the PRD.

The simple drone named Crop Squad is designed for agriculture applications and is expected to monitor crops, analyze the local crop health, and upload the reports or upload the raw capture to the datacenter for further analysis. From the mechanical engineering perspective, there are specific things to take care of for this drone.

What are the typical mechanical requirements of Crop Squad to fulfill this application?

1. A quadcopter to fly high to cover or get a view of a larger area of the agricultural land

2. A hyperspectral imaging camera to capture the patterns or other observations of the crops (leaves, stems, and pods) periodically

3. A high-speed wireless network to upload the raw image capture back to the datacenter for further processing and analysis or to analyze locally if the drone is equipped with a high computing processor

4. A remote controller to operate the drone from a remote location or equip the drone with artificial intelligence (AI) to do the job independently without any control

At a high level, the requirement looks simple, with four variables: quadcopter, camera, wireless network, and remote. But creating a mechanical design is not as simple as that; numerous variables come into the picture. The mechanical design also depends on the creativity of the individuals. While the form factor or aesthetics of a product (including a drone) are driven by industrial design and marketing, design engineers usually have to apply a lot of creativity and ideas of innovation in meeting the requirements.

Figure 2-3 shows the different types of mechanical designs that can be created for the requirements mentioned above. Each drone design is unique and it's up to designer to decide which design best suits their application.

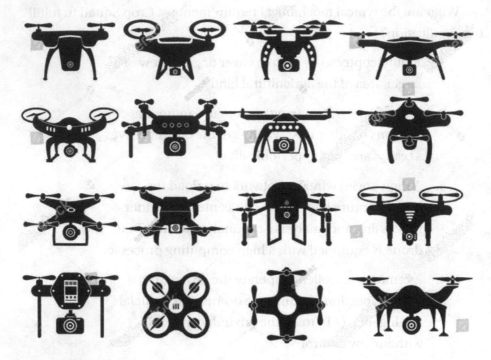

Figure 2-3. *Possible mechanical design variants*

Definition

The mechanical design is defined as an industrial design (ID). Mass production can be done only in the factory automation tooling process, because the activity is often a completely repetitive process. This means the design should be predefined as per the manufacturability of factory standards and the factory should be prepared for the manufacturing process for the application-specific ID.

As a part of the ID selection, the choice of materials is important because the factory must be able to handle those materials in the process. For example, the manufacturing process is completely different for metal or plastic, so the factory needs to prepare differently for metal or plastic.

An X-frame of the drone can be made from plastic or metal. A plastic part and a metal part need to be designed differently, and the factory process is likely to change based on the material.

With all other things being the same, the ID is one of the key deciding factors since it creates the first impression with the customers, and a favorable impression increases product sales.

Purpose

The PRD lists the high-level applications of the drone. It's the engineer's responsibility to learn the next level of details and understand the actual purpose of the drone. For example, Agriculture is the broad area where drones are used for soil and field analysis; to spray the seeds; and to irrigate, monitor, and collect health report of the crops.

If a single drone is designed for all of the above mentioned purpose, the ID and system design will be complex. Even if the system is designed to perform all of these tasks, the design will overload and the system CPU unit may not support multiple parallel activities with the current available technology. Instead, a single drone can be designed to fulfill a combination of two or three applications together. The engineer has to clearly mark the abilities of the drone being built.

Figure 2-4 shows the drone mounted with a hyperspectral camera used to monitor crops. The same drone cannot be used for soil and field analysis and for spraying water or seeds unless equipped with relevant modules inside.

Figure 2-4. *An agriculture drone used to monitor crops*

Requirements

Once the purpose is known, the engineer can convert the PRD to next-level detailed mechanical requirements for an ID, including hardware and software.

The PRD and the purpose trigger the engineer's creativity and give birth to a brand new drone design. The engineer works with a cross-functional team for the materials required, size, and shape of the ID.

The PCBA is considered as a single mechanical part from the hardware team. The dimensions of the PCB are the most important requirements from the hardware engineers to complete an ID. Some other requirements are battery dimension, antenna position, and IO connector placement.

Figure 2-5 shows the typical stack-up of mechanical parts in a drone ID. This is also the cross-sectional view of the mechanical design of the drone, and the significance of each part is explained below. This stack-up may differ for drones in different applications.

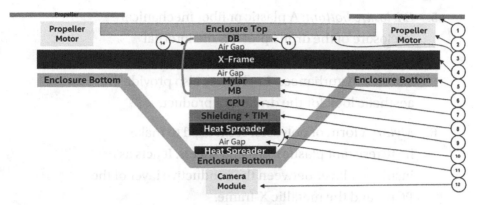

Figure 2-5. *A typical drone system stack-up*

1. *Propeller*: Angled blades attached to the revolving shaft of a motor. These blades gives thrust and are why the drones can fly high.

2. *Propeller motor*: This is a DC motor attached to the four corners of the X-Frame. Power from the drone's electrical system rotates the blades to provide thrust to the drone.

3. *Enclosure top*: A plastic or fiber mechanical enclosure of the drone protects the internal electrical and mechanical subsystems from the external disturbances. Enclosures also provide the aesthetic look for the drone as a product.

4. *X-frame*: This is the vertebra of the drone. All of the other mechanical parts and subsystems of the drone are attached to the X-frame through different types of fasteners or ties. The X-frame is symmetrical by dimensions and weight on all sides to achieve a balanced flight of the drone. So the cross-sectional view is symmetrical on Y axis.

5. *Enclosure bottom*: A plastic or fiber mechanical enclosure of the drone protects the internal electrical and mechanical subsystems from the external disturbances. Enclosures also provide the aesthetic look for the drone as a product.

6. *Mylar*: A form of polyester resin used to make heat-resistant plastic films and sheets. It acts as an insulation layer between the conductive layer of the PCBA and the metallic X-frame.

7. *MB (motherboard)*: The PCBA of the system hosts all of the electrical parts of the system soldered on to it. By modifying the PCBA shape, the same layer can accommodate the battery on the sides of the PCBA.

8. *CPU*: Usually an SOC, it's the processing unit of the system. All other devices soldered on the PCBA are on the same layer adjacent to the CPU.

9. *Shielding and TIM*: Digital and RF devices usually need shielding to protect from external disturbances or to protect the external devices through radiation. Radiation from the external world is suppressed by connecting the shield to a system ground.

    The TIM, thermal interface materials such as graphite, is pasted as a thin layer on the shield to radiate the excess heat generated from the components of the system.

10. *Heat spreader*: The heat exchanger that moves heat between a heat source and a secondary heat exchange, whose surface area and geometry are more favorable than the source.

11.   *Air gap*: Provided wherever necessary in a
      system. This air gap acts an insulator and also
      accommodates material expansion and contraction
      due to unavoidable reasons in a system.

12.   *Camera module*: The lower-most part of the
      drone in this application is the camera module.
      Attached on the bottom to get a better field of view
      (FOV) when drone fly high. Most camera modules
      accommodate ISPs and connect to the SOC through
      the USB 3.1 interface. If the SOC has integrated ISPs,
      then the camera sensor can directly connect to the
      SOC with camera-specific interfaces.

13.   *DB (daughterboard)*: If all of the ingredients can't
      be accommodated in the single PCBA, then there
      can be several daughterboards on the system to
      accommodate additional ingredients. Motherboards
      and daughterboards can be connected through
      board-to-board interconnections or a flex PCB
      interconnect. In this drone, the WiFi+BT module
      cannot be kept below the X-frame. The metal
      X-frame might obstruct the signal for the module's
      embedded antenna. Alternatively, the module can
      be kept in the same PCBA with the external antenna,
      which may not be good for an ID.

14.   *FPC (flexible PCB)*: Generally used to connect one
      or more rigid PCBs in a complex system.

Dependencies

Although the engineer's creativity and ideas produce an attractive ID, the discrete components, subsystem location, and other dependencies can limit her ideas from becoming a reality.

Multiple discrete components such as the X-frame, motors, propellers, PCBA, screws, gaskets, enclosures, batteries, FPCs, and cables integrate through various electrical and mechanical interconnects in an ID. Apart from the discrete mechanical components, there are electrical subsystems located on the PCBA, which largely impact the design of the ID.

For example, the position of the power and IO connectors determine the front, back, top, and bottom view of the ID. Usually IO connectors are placed on the back or bottom side of the ID to make them invisible to the user. Also, the presence of wireless components prominently affects the ID design. The antenna is the most vital part of the wireless interface and its placement varies for the mobile network, WiFi, and other RF remote control technologies.

With all of the above mentioned challenges, the mechanical team has to come up with best ID for the product.

Hardware Design

The process of converting the Figure 2-2 block diagram or hardware architecture to a fully functional PCBA is called hardware design. The hardware design fundamentally focuses on getting the desired functionality to the system. PCBA development starts with the hardware requirement capture based on the PRD, followed by ingredients selection and choice of the right PCB to interconnect the ingredients, and finally, the power architecture, design, and implementation for the hardware.

The PCBA is considered as a single discrete mechanical part in an ID. Subsystems and other ingredients of the PCBA are part of the electrical BOM.

Hardware Requirements

The first step in hardware design is the understanding of the hardware requirements. Hardware requirements may vary depending on the operating system and the overall system design, which is usually covered in the PRD.

There are variations possible for a system providing similar functionality. For our case, there could be different variations of drones possible, but still providing the functionality we outlined. The differentiation comes from the parts that are chosen in the system. Generally speaking, there are different modules that can provide certain functionality. However, there may be differences relating to, for example, the power, performance, latency, and durability of those components.

Generally, there are minimum hardware specifications of the devices, which barely meet the requirements. If the system is built with these devices, it's a low-end product. A low-end product usually lacks speed and quality. So it is the one of the cheapest in the product range or on the market as a whole.

Above minimum requirements, there are recommended specifications for the effective operation of the operating system. Products with these specifications fall in the medium range in terms of cost and quality.

Also, there is a higher end to the hardware specifications of each device, under which the system will operate at high performance. So the product is one of the most expensive or advanced in a product range or on the market as a whole.

It is typically the hardware or the devices used that define whether the system is a low-end or high-end product. Table 2-2 shows the hardware requirements of the drone.

Table 2-2. *Drone Hardware Requirements*

Features	Key Component Requirement	Proposals	Dependencies
CPU	Quad-core 2.34 GHz	Quad-core 2.34GHz	Required
Memory	2GB LPDDR3	4GB LPDDR3	Required
Storage	64 GB uSSD	128GB uSSD	Required
Camera	600-975nm, line scan, hyperspectral imaging	470-900nm, line scan, hyperspectral imaging	Required
WiFi	802.11 1x1 ac module	M.2 12*16 802.11 1x1 ac module	Required
Sensor	Accelerometer, ambient light, gyroscope, temperature, altitude, pressure	Accelerometer, ambient light, gyroscope, temperature, altitude, pressure	Required
IO ports	1xUSB Type C 1xuSD4.0 1xuSIM 1xPowerJack		Required
Mobile Network	LTE	M.2 LTE Module	Optional
FPGA			
PCB	12-Layer HDI	8-Layer HDI	Required
Power	Integrated	Integrated	Required
Charger	7.4V, 5A	7.4V, 5A	Required
Battery	10000mAHr	10000mAHr	Required
DC adapter	12V, 3A	12V, 3A	Required

Electrical Ingredients Selection

As explained in Chapter 1, the detailed electrical feature set of the system is directly related to the electrical ingredients of the PCBA. Selection of ingredients is based on the detailed analysis of the current available technologies and anticipated technological developments. Usually, the ingredients supplied by different vendors vary in terms of cost, package, technology, and lead time based on factory production capabilities.

All the ingredients selected should adhere to the technology used in the SOC. The SOC as a central processing unit connects all the ingredients as peripherals of the system. Table 2-1 shows the list of electrical ingredients of the system. The same list will become the key component of the bill of materials, with the addition of the manufacturer and manufacturer part number details.

BOM and Component Procurement

The bill of materials is a list of components required to build a system or product. It includes raw materials, subassemblies, intermediate assemblies, subcomponents, parts, and the quantities of each needed to manufacture an end product. A component may be used for communication between manufacturing partners, or confined to a single manufacturing plant. A bill of materials is often tied to a production order whose issuance may generate reservations for components in the bill of materials that are in stock and requisitions for components that are not in stock.

The list of materials required to build a system or a product is called a system BOM. A system BOM is usually hierarchical in nature with multiple levels. Each component in a BOM or subassembly in the main can be called a child item of the main BOM.

Similarly, the list of components or materials required to build a PCBA is called an electrical BOM (EBOM). The EBOM is a part of the system BOM in most systems and is one of the child items of the main BOM.

In general, the electrical components are selected based on the following key parameters:

- Availability: Availability is usually a development schedule of the part. Design, build date, quantity, and lead time of the part should match the project schedule.

- Production status: The production status should be active when the final product is built. Inactive or end-of-life (EOL) samples are recommended for a new design. At the very least, engineering samples should be available during the design phase, if not production samples.

- Cost: Cost is a key factor to be negotiated with the manufacturer to get the overall target BOM cost as low as possible.

- Operating temperature: Each ingredient falls under different temperature grades like commercial, industrial, and defense. The cost will increase if the operating temperature range increases.

Note The widely accepted operating temperature range for commercial is – 0 to 60, for industrial is -40 to 85, and for military is -55 to 125.

- Storage temperature: The temperature at which devices/products are stored, typically ambient temperature.

All of the parts shown in Figure 2-5 are child items of the system BOM. Reservations should be placed for the parts that need to be procured from the third party-vendors. Custom-built parts like the X-frame, enclosures, head spreader, PCBA, etc. are done at the OEM/ODM factory facility by preparing the factory specific to the drone project.

An OEM (original equipment manufacturer) is a company that manufactures the drone; it is marketed with a different manufacturer's name.

An ODM (original design manufacturer) is a company that designs and manufactures the product as per the specifications; the product is rebranded by another company for sale.

PCBA Design

The PCBA design is the extended process in the system design. Some degree of pre-work needs to be done during the architecture phase. More details will be explained in the upcoming chapters

To select the right PCB for a system, the following parameters need to be examined:

1. PCBA dimensions

2. PCB type

3. PCB layer stack-up

PCBA Dimensions

The target length, width, and thickness of the PCBA are derived from the mechanical design. All of the ingredients need to be accommodated in the given length, width, and height of the PCB. Figure 2-6 illustrates the PCBA dimension.

In this design, the Crop Squad drone is the size of a mid-sized commercial drone. This PCB is approximately less than a size of the credit card, which is 85mm X 54mm. The target PCB dimensions slightly vary based on the final ID design from the mechanical engineers. The thin red line in the figure is the outline of the PCBA, from which the dimensions are marked as XXmm. It is actually a top view of the PCBA showing the footprints of the components placed on the top side. The PCBA and footprints are created using a PCB CAD tool.

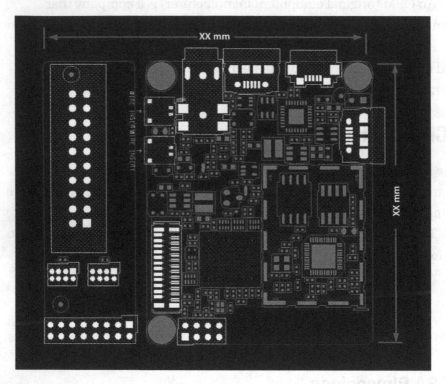

Figure 2-6. *PCBA dimensions*

PCB Type

Different types of PCBs can be used in a system. Common PCBs are

1. Rigid

2. Flex

3. Hybrid (`rigid-flex`)

Rigid PCBs are most preferred. Flex PCBs are used in a complex systems where rigid PCBs do not fit.

In the Crop Squad drone, shown in Figure 2-1, the architecture diagram of the SSD and WiFi Bluetooth modules are placed on a separate board and are connected to the main board through a FPC connector. This shows that the electrical part of the drone is split into two rigid PCBAs connected through a flexible PCB. The idea is to keep the WiFi module on a separate PCB to avoid the obstruction of the embedded antenna by the metallic X-frame and to eliminate the need of any external antenna.

In some systems, a rigid PCB breaks into small pieces and is interconnected through the flexible PCBs without any external interconnect, which is also called a hybrid PCB.

Figure 2-7 shows two rigid PCBs interconnected with a flexible PCB. This figure clearly shows that rigid PCBs cannot be folded, whereas flex PCBs can be folded any direction with minimum bend radius.

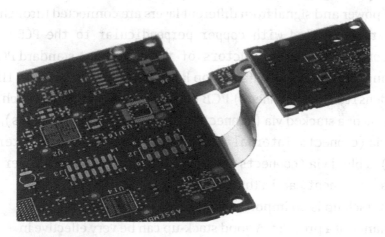

Figure 2-7. *Hybrid PCB*

Layer Stack-Up

A PCB can be single-sided or double-sided. A single-sided PCB is one that has components placed on one side (top or bottom), whereas a double-sided PCB has components on both the top and bottom side. The advantages of a single-side PCB is low cost manufacturing and easy assembly. No air gap is required for the non-component side inside a mechanical assembly. The manufacturability and assembly cost is high for a double-sided assembly and an air gap is required on both sides in a mechanical assembly, since both sides are mounted with components.

In a complicated system, multiple conductive and dielectric layers are sandwiched and laminated in between. Layer count, copper plane, and dielectric thickness decide the overall thickness of the PCB.

The number of power rails in a system is directly proportional to the power layer count. Signal count, trace width, and density of the high speed and low speed signals determine the signal layer count of the PCB.

The power and signal from different layers are connected through "vias" (drills filled with copper perpendicular to the PCB plane connecting the conductors of the layers). A standard PCB has through hole vias covering the top layer to the bottom layer. An HDI (high-density interconnect) PCB has multiple via structures such as a micro via or a stacked via (connects only two adjacent layers), a buried via (connects internal layers not exposed to any external layers), a blind via (connects the top layer to the next layer under a component) and a through hole via.

PCB stack-up is an important factor in determining the EMC performance of a product. A good stack-up can be very effective in reducing radiation from the loops on the PCB (differential-mode emission), as well as the cables attached to the board (common-mode emission). On the other hand, a poor stack-up can increase the radiation from both of these mechanisms considerably.

Figure 2-8 shows partial layer stack up of 3-6-3+ PCB with buried vias (4-9) connecting 6 internal layers, a through hole via (1-12) connecting all 16 layers, and a micro via or stacked via connecting the adjacent layers for the top 4 and bottom 4 layers. The first column of the table shows the layer name (i.e. signal or power). The signal layer is the layer in which the actual signal with specific impedance is routed. The power layer is made up of one or more copper planes that carry different power supplies for ICs on the PCBA. The second column shows the layer type. The layer type is either a conductive layer with thickness mentioned in ounces along with conductive plating as "1/3oz+plating" or a dielectric layer with material properties mentioned as "PP1067/1078." The other two columns show the thickness of each layer and tolerance in millimeters. The last column in the stack-up is the dielectric constant of the dielectric materials. In general, the stack-up will have a few more columns, including the trace width of the signal to achieve the target impedances.

A detailed feasibility study needs to be done to select the right PCB layer stack-up. Usually floor planning along with a route study is done with a minimum layer count by the combined effort of electrical design engineers and CAD engineers to arrive the right stack-up.

In Figure 2-2, there are high-speed electrical connections on the PCB such SATA, USB3.1, HDMI, and PCIE. Considering the size of the board and the density of the high-speed signal, the design may require 6 signal layers and 6 power layers based on the initial assessment.

Via arrangements are decided based on the signal and power layer arrangement. In this stack-up, the top 4 and bottom 4 layers can be interconnected though a micro via. The 3-x-3+ mentioned in the stack-up is a micro via on the first and last 3 layers plus an additional layer. Then the center x number of layers are connected though a buried via.

Cost is an important factor and plays a key role in deciding the stack-up. So many factors affect the cost of a PCB; for example, in the layer stack-up in Figure 2-8 there will be significant cost reduction by reducing the layer count, via pattern (removing the blind and buried vias will significantly reduce manufacturing cost). It is up to the designer to choose the optimum and correct stack-up for the design. The PCB stack can be changed throughout the hardware design phase before we release the design files for PCB fabrication. These PCB fabrication files also called Gerber files. More details on this in upcoming chapters.

Layer name	Layer type	Finished (mm)	tolerance(mm)	Permittivity (Er) 1GHZ
S/M		0.030		
TOP (Sig/PWR/GND)	1/3oz+plating	0.033	+/-0.010	
	PP1067/1078	0.068	+/-0.015	3.5~3.8
L2 (GND)	1/3oz+plating	0.030	+/-0.010	
	PP1067/1078	0.065	+/-0.015	3.5~3.8
L3(Sig/PWR/GND)	1/3oz+plating	0.022	+/-0.010	
	PP1067/1078	0.068	+/-0.015	3.5~3.8
L4(Sig/PWR/GND)	1/3oz+plating	0.035	+/-0.010	
	PP1067/1078	0.065	+/-0.015	3.5~3.8
L5(Sig/PWR/GND)	H oz	0.017	+/-0.010	
	core	0.064	+/-0.015	3.5~3.8
L6(Sig/PWR/GND)	H oz	0.017	+/-0.010	
	core 14mil+PP	0.610	+/-0.060	3.5~3.8
L7(Sig)	H oz	0.017	+/-0.010	
	core	0.064	+/-0.015	3.5~3.8
L8(GND)	H oz	0.017	+/-0.010	
	PP1067/1078	0.065	+/-0.015	3.5~3.8
L9(Sig)	1/3oz+plating	0.035	+/-0.010	
	PP1067/1078	0.068	+/-0.015	3.5~3.8
L10(GND)	1/3oz+plating	0.022	+/-0.010	
	PP1067/1078	0.065	+/-0.015	3.5~3.8
L11(Sig/PWR/GND)	1/3oz+plating	0.030	+/-0.010	
	PP1067/1078	0.068	+/-0.015	3.5~3.8
BOT (Sig/PWR/GND)	1/3oz+plating	0.033	+/-0.010	
S/M		0.030		
		1.638		

Figure 2-8. PCB layer stack-up

Floor Plan

Placement of the electrical ingredients on a given PCB area is controlled by SOC placement. SOC interfaces are distributed in such a way that they connect the ingredients that are placed around. All of the ingredients placed around the SOC need to be connected with shorter traces due to restrictions in the routed interface length. Figure 2-9 shows a typical floor plan of a PCB with the SOC in the center and other electrical ingredients around. (The floor plan shown is only for illustration purposes and does not correspond to the drone architecture in Figure 2-2.)

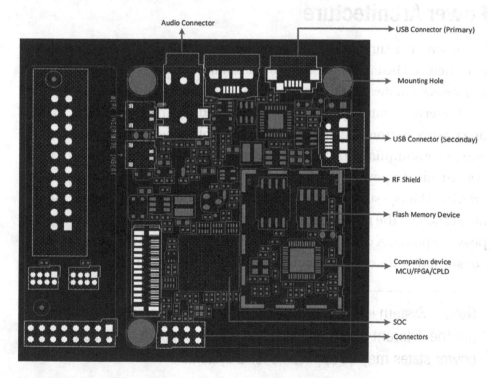

Figure 2-9. *SOC, peripheral device, and connector placement*

The floor plan also includes the height of the PCB, a major dependency for the mechanical design. Electrical ingredients placed on a PCB vary in height, and the mechanical design needs to account for each and every component. Generally, inductors and capacitors are the tallest electrical components in the PCBA. Also, high-power consumption devices dissipate more heat, and these power dissipating devices need cooling systems. The cooling systems, such as heat sinks and fans, are the non-electrics parts considered part of the PCBA and they add to the overall height of the PCBA.

Power Architecture

The energy consumption and the battery life have become critical system parameters. The early estimation of maximum system power consumption is necessary to design a more efficient power supply.

Battery-operated systems generally have different power states. This power state is more specific to the use cases of drones. Drone system power consumption drastically varies for each power states. Drone system idle is a power state in which all subsystems are on, without any activity. This is a state where the drone is grounded and thus not in the air. Standby is the power state in which the system consumes the lowest possible power. A drone in flight with video recording is the highest power consumption state and it drains the battery at the fastest rate.

Note   System idle, active flight, video recording, sleep, and standby are the different power states a system can support. Not all the power states may be applicable for a system.

The power map is the simple representation of the power architecture. Generally, the power map represents only the maximum power consumption state of the system.

Power Estimation

In any hardware design, the components in the PCBA are broadly classified as active and passive devices. Active devices are the components that consume energy. All ICs are active devices whereas inductors, capacitors, resistors, and diodes are passive devices that do not need any power for operation. ICs such as SOCs and other subsystem devices need more than one power supply (also called a power rail). Generally ICs have a core rail and IO rails, and core rails consume more power than IO rails. More details on the power consumption of the devices are discussed in following chapters.

The power consumption details of each device need to be extracted from the datasheet of the device. The datasheet states the absolute and recommended maximum voltage and current specs of the device for all power states.

In most designs, the number of power rails required for the platform is equal to or more than the required rails of SOC. Considering the SOC and platform requirements are equally complicated and the design demands different power sequencing for the SOC and the platform. Keeping the SOC and platform requirements separate will make the calculation simple.

SOC Power Requirements

Table 2-3 shows the SOC voltage and current requirements. The SOC itself as system on chip with multiple functional unit blocks requires different voltage and current to operate. A typical SOC has functional unit blocks such as core, graphics, memory, clock, PLL, display, camera, high-speed IO, low-speed IO, etc. Each block's voltage range and current consumption is listed in the table.

Appropriate power devices need to be selected based on the voltage and current requirement. The power supply should meet the voltage tolerance (±5% for 3.3V and ±3% for 1.8V) level mentioned in the datasheet

45

of the each device. The power supply design should accommodate the appropriate filter circuits to eliminate the ripple and noise from the power supply before feeding into the devices. Ripple and noise can be reduced by arranging the power layers in the stack-up as well. Other ways of reducing the ripple are by placing the power components in the right location and implementing the best-known power routing techniques.

In new generation SOCs, each functional unit block can be individually power-gated, which means if any block is unused or inactive, it can be switched off completely to save power.

Table 2-3. *SOC Voltage and Current Requirements*

SOC Power	3.3V ±5%	1.8V ±3%	1.35V ±3%	1.2V ±3%	1.0V ±3%	0.7–1.1V
Core						3000
Graphics						5000
Logic						1800
L2/L3					2200	
Memory				1200		
Display IO	300			300		
CFIO		500		200		
SDIO	93					
USB	200					
TOTAL	593	500	1200	500	2200	9800

Platform Power Requirements

Similar to the SOC, there are multiple other devices on the platform that have different voltage and current requirements. These devices spread across the platform, and the few devices requiring common voltage can be switched on simultaneously without any sequencing. Table 2-4 shows the platform voltage and current requirements.

Multiple subsystems need same the voltage. For example, display, sensors, camera, and modem are different subsystems and require common 3.3V with different current requirements and with no specific sequencing (all the subsystems can be switched on simultaneously).

The platform has multiple power gates for each device to enable/disable power for the device when not in operation, similar to the SOC, where each block can be power-gated internally to save power.

Table 2-4. *Platform Voltage and Current Requirements*

Subsystem	Ingredients	5.0V	3.3V	1.8V	1.35V	1.2V
MEMORY	LPDDR3					1200
STORAGE	uSSD			300		
UI	Display,		100			
	camera,	900				
	sensors		10	10		
COMMS	Modem,		500			
	GPS		150			
	Wi-Fi/BT,		400			
FPGA	FPGA		500			
USB	2.0, 3.0	1400				
TOTAL		2300	1760	310	0	1200

Power Devices

The previous section listed the voltage, current, ripple, and noise requirements for the SOC and platform. The total number of voltage rails for the SOC and platform combined and the total calculated current consumption for each rail in the SOC and platform helps the engineer to choose the right power devices for the system. Most power devices fall into two categories: linear and switching regulators.

Linear Regulators

A linear regulator operates by using a voltage-controlled source to force a fixed voltage to appear at the regulator output terminal. The most commonly used linear regulator is the low dropout (LDO) regulator. The difference between the input voltage and the generated output voltage is the dropout voltage. The product of the dropout voltage and the current consumed by the device at the output of the regulator is the power dissipated at the source. Basically, low dropout voltage and less current consumption are the desirable parameters when selecting an LDO.

Switching Regulators

Switching regulators operate by switching on/off a series of devices. A FET will be switched on/off by a pulse width modulation (PWM) controller transferring energy to load. When the switch is on, energy is stored on an inductor and capacitor and is also supplying to load. When the switch is off, the stored energy is discharged to the load until the voltage reaches the minimum required threshold of the load device. The on/off is done in a specific duty cycle to keep the output voltage within the tolerance level of the load device. There are different types of switching regulators: buck, boost, and buck boost regulators.

Choosing the Best Regulator

The best regulator can be determined by evaluating the parameters listed in Table 2-5.

Table 2-5. *Comparison of Linear and Switching Reguators*

Parameters	Linear	Switching
Function	Only steps down. Input voltage must not be greater than the output voltage.	Step up, step down, and inverts
Efficiency	Low to medium	High
Complexity	Low	Medium to high
Size	Small to medium	Large
Cost	Low	Medium to high
Ripple/noise	Low	Medium to high

Function: Most designs convert high voltage to low voltage. Buck is desirable, and can be either a linear or switching regulator. If any design demands low voltage to high voltage conversion, then the regulator choice is a switching regulator. For example, USB powered systems have 5.0 volts as the main input, but some systems, like displaying black light, need a higher voltage to operate. In this case, a boost regulator is required to up-convert this 5.0 to a higher voltage.

Efficiency: There is no control over the efficiency of the linear regulator. The product of the load current and the difference in the input and output voltage gives the power dissipation of the device. For this reason, linear regulators cannot be used for high load current (the load current limit depends on the dropout voltage and max thermal dissipation of the device). But switching regulators can be used for higher current loads and efficiency can be increased by carefully selecting the external components

49

like low RDS on MOSFETs, low DCR inductors, and low ESR capacitors. For better efficiency, go for switching regulators.

Complexity: A linear regulator is very simple. Less external components are required for stable operation and easy implementation, whereas the switching regulators are complex, due to the external components dependencies. More accurate calculations are required when selecting the components for stable operation.

Size: Linear regulators occupy less space in the board, while switching regulators need more space on the board to accommodate the PWM controller, external MOSFETs, inductors, capacitors, and other analog components.

Cost: The architecture of the linear regulator is simple so the cost is less. The switching regulator cost is high considering its advantages of high current and better efficiency in a complex device architecture. On top of the device cost, the switching regulator needs external components for normal operation, so the overall cost is multiple times higher than that of a linear regulator.

Ripple/noise: Ripple and noise are lower in a linear regulator; this quality makes the linear regulator more suitable for analog designs and clock and PLL blocks in the SOC. Switching regulator outputs are noisier than linear ones even with multistage filters.

Power Map

The previous section explained the pros and cons of the switching and linear regulators. Linear or switching regulators need to be selected for multiple power rails of the SOC and platform. Among the power rails, some need to be always on and some need to be power-gated whenever the system goes to sleep or the subsystem is inactive for some reason. Also, there are different power sequencing requirements for the SOC, platform, and other devices if specified in the datasheet.

All of the requirements for power consumption, power gating, and sequencing on a power map are drawn for easy understanding and are converted to an actual design of circuits. Figure 2-10 illustrates the power map, which will be converted to power design in schematics and then into a PCBA.

Generally, the initial power map may not be accurate with the drone architecture. It may go through significant changes on the later part of the design based on the requirements of the electrical specifications of the ingredients. A very complicated power architecture can be explained in a simple way using a power map. From a landscape view, the items on the left are

1. *Source* is the type of regulator used to deliver the power. For example, Buck, Buck1... Buck6 are switching regulators used to deliver higher load currents delivering multiple loads together. ALDO, DLDO, and GPLDO are LDOs delivering lower currents either for single load or multiple loads.

2. *Rail Name* is the name of the connection used on the board to differentiate from one another. Multiple 3.3V will be delivered from multiple sources to multiple loads. Connections should be used to distinguish names to avoid a short circuit on the PCBA.

3. *Voltage* is the voltage level or the range the source is delivering.

4. *Imax* is the maximum load current the device will support or specified by the vendor in the datasheet.

5. *Iload* is the maximum current the device is actually loaded by the subsystem connected to in the design.

On the top side of the power map are the details of the SOC blocks and subsystems (camera, display, memory, modem, etc.); current consumptions are listed. The power map also shows the connections from the power supply devices to the subsystems and distribution along the platform. The representation of power distribution in a map makes the conversion easy for schematics and layout. Every connection in the power map will become a trace on a PCB. The current consumption values mentioned in the power map will help to calculate the power plane thickness and power trace width in PCB.

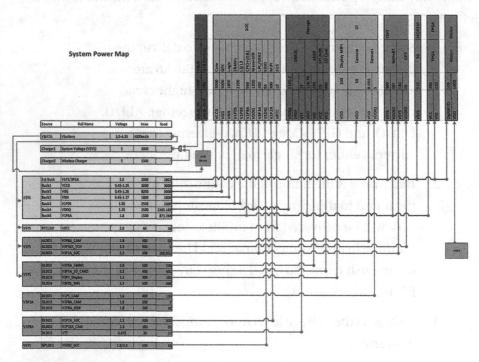

Figure 2-10. *System power map*

Power Sequencing

Powering up a circuit on a printed circuit board is too often taken for granted and can cause damage and both destructive and nondestructive latch-up conditions. These problems may not be prominent until volume production begins, when the tolerances of devices and designs are put to the test. This is dangerously late in the process and extremely expensive with respect to time and the delivery of projects and products. Errors found at this stage result in numerous modifications, including PCB layout changes, design alterations, and extra anomalies. With the advent of incorporating many functional blocks into one integrated circuit (IC), this results in supplying these blocks with multiple, sometimes equal, or in many instances, differing voltage supplies. As more and more of these SoC ICs proliferate the marketplace, the need for particular power supply sequencing and power management issues arises. There is usually enough information on device datasheets to guide a designer to a correct power-up sequence for an individual IC. However, some ICs specifically require a well-defined power-up sequence. This is true in the case of many of ICs and is quite common in ones using multiple supplies such as converters (consisting of both analog-to-digital converters (ADCs) and digital-to-analog converters (DACs)), digital signal processors (DSPs), audio/video, radio frequency, and many other mixed signal ICs. Essentially, any IC containing some analog input/output with a digital engine falls into this category, where particular power sequencing may be required. On these ICs, there could be separate analog and digital supplies and some may even have a digital input/output supply, as detailed in specific examples discussed in the following sections. Some of the more common supplies presently are +1.8 V, +2.0 V, +2.5 V, +3.3 V, +5 V, −5 V, +12 V, and −12 V.

Figure 2-11 shows a typical power sequencing requirement of the SOC. Table 2-6 shows the timing details of the each power in microseconds.

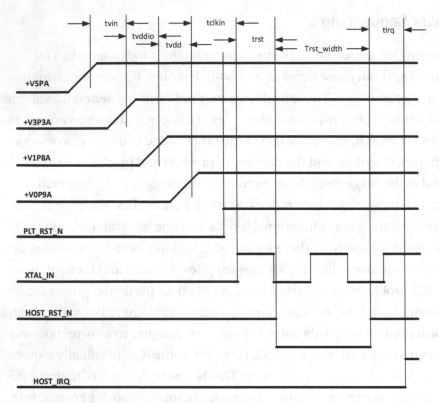

Figure 2-11. *SOC power-on sequence*

Table 2-6. *SOC Power Sequencing Numbers*

Symbol	Description	Min	Max	Units
Tvin	+V3P3A stable power after +5PA USB power	0	NA	us
Tvddio	+V1P8A stable power after +3P3A	100	NA	us
Tvdd	+V0P9A stable power after +V1P8A	100	300	us
Tclkin	Clock active after +V0P9A stable	100	NA	us
Trst	Host reset assertion after clock	10	NA	us
Trst_Width	Host reset active time	10	NA	us
Tirq	Host interrupt assertion after deassertion of Host rest	50	200	us

Battery Estimation

Batteries are energy storage devices that are particularly useful for powering small portable devices like phones, laptops, and entertainment devices as well as mobility devices that travel over the Earth's surface, through water, and in the air.

Battery Constraints

The batteries used in these applications are engineered to meet the unique design constraints imposed by these different applications. These constraints are covered in the following sections.

Number of Cells or Voltage

The term "battery" refers to a system of one or more cells. A cell represents a particular chemical combination capable of producing a voltage and a current. Different chemical combinations produce different voltages. By combining cells in series, the voltage of a battery pack can be increased as a multiple of the number of cells x the voltage of each cell.

Battery Chemistry

A rechargeable battery is referred to as a storage battery and is usually constructed of one or more secondary cells. Each cell is capable of producing a specific voltage with respect to the electrochemical makeup of the cell. Batteries store energy through changes in their internal chemistry. When a battery is discharged through a load like a circuit or a motor, the internal battery chemistry undergoes a change. When the battery is charged, the chemical change is reversed, and the energy is again stored in the battery. A specific amount of energy can be stored in a battery given the specific battery chemistry, the configuration of the battery, and the battery volume and weight.

Cell Voltage and Battery Packs

For NiCad/NiMH, cell voltage is about 1.2V; for lead acid, it is 2.0V; and for lithium cells, it is on the order of 3.6V. Typically, portable electronic devices are designed to run on 12, 24, 36, or 48 voltages. To create these voltages, a number of cells are connected in series in order to form a battery that has the desired net voltage.

Battery Capacity

Battery capacity is published by the manufacturer as a nominal rating for a given set of discharge conditions. These discharge conditions include rate of discharge (C rate), temperature, and minimum cell voltage. Minimum cell voltage is the lowest voltage to which a cell or battery should be charged. Discharging a cell or a battery below the minimum voltage can reduce or even destroy the battery's capacity to hold a charge.

Battery performance parameters can include voltage, amp-hour capacity, and C rate (rate of discharge).

The C rate refers to the amount of current the battery can sustain for an hour while remaining within a specified voltage range. For a typical 12 volt battery, this voltage range is between 12 volts and 10.5 volts for the battery to be considered fully charged.

Typical units of battery capacity are expressed as a milliamp-hours or mA*h; for larger batteries, it is amp-hours or A*h. This rating implies the discharge rate in amperes that the battery can be expected to sustain for a period of one hour.

Battery capacity varies with the discharge rate. When you discharge a battery at higher rates, the amp-hour capacity of the battery will be less than the nominal or published capacity.

Battery capacity is measured in amp-hours (Ah). A pack that can deliver 1 amp for 1 hour has a capacity of 1 Ah. The battery capacity is usually given by the manufacturer in amp hours (Ah) or milliamp hours (mAh).

Suppose a 15lb drone with four motors draws an average of 4 amps for video recording on the flight. If you fit a 4 Ah battery pack, it can be expected to run for one hour on average.

Watt Hours and Energy Density

There are two different ways of indicating battery capacity: you can use either AHr (ampere hour) or WHr (watt hour) for battery life calculations. And both approaches are used in product designs. The WHr approach is more comprehensible. The watt-hours stored in a battery pack are approximated by multiplying the rated amp-hours by the pack voltage.

Energy density usually refers to the energy in watt hours per unit mass of the battery. The energy available from a given battery can be estimated using the manufacturer's published data for a given battery pack or cell. The information needed to calculate the energy density can also be obtained through direct battery testing. Battery energy is described in units of watt-hours/kilogram.

Battery Cost

Each battery chemistry requires a specific type of charge and charge regime. Battery chemistries and chargers vary in both initial cost and lifetime costs. Lithium-based batteries present higher initial costs than similar capacity batteries employing other chemistries. However, lithium batteries have high energy densities, long life cycles, and are more readily recyclable than other chemistries. These factors contribute to lower lifetime costs.

There is no answer to the question, "What is the best battery system I can buy?" The answer always depends on the many factors involved in a particular application. Battery systems and chemistries can be cost compared using the relationship cost/watt-hr. Low cost/watt-hr figures can indicate cost-effective energy storage.

This is precisely why designers and engineers need to have skills and knowledge to analyze battery regimes in order to make the best selection for a particular application.

For example, a battery used in a drone must have a high energy-to-weight ratio. This would imply an investigation into lithium battery technology. Battery systems can be expensive. It is therefore necessary to make careful evaluations of the requirements and constraints imposed by a particular application.

Software Architecture

Software is the driver (in a way) of a system. In other words, the hardware provides the capabilities, while the software uses the same, makes it run, and provides the desired functionality. Theoretically speaking, there is always a possibility to design purpose-built hardware(with limited or no software) for a particular usage; however, practically speaking, we need to make design decisions in terms of what functionality should be part of hardware and what should be part of software. These design decisions are made very early in the requirement phase. And, once done, the hardware and software system designs run in parallel. Of course, there is some dependency of SW development (and testing) on HW availability. However, the dependency is mitigated by means of using HW simulators. The simulators are used to provide the functional models of hardware, which can be used to run and validate the software.

As discussed in the previous chapter, there are various different categories to the SW stack. In this section, we talk about each category and how and when they are developed.

1. Firmware components: You know that the firmware components are dependent on and tied to the device they are associated with. The device vendor is responsible for providing production-worthy

firmware for the device. In this section, the term "device" also includes the SoC.

2. OS and drivers: The OS component is supplied by the OSV (OS vendors). There are a number of OS flavors and variations that we can choose from. This decision is guided by the OS properties and characteristics. For our example, we'll use a real-time operating system, since drones are real-time devices. The drivers fall into two categories. The drivers for generic devices based on a certain standard can be part of the OS itself, as an inbox component. However, the drivers for devices with differentiated values and characteristics are provided by the device vendor itself. As the choices relating to hardware devices to be used on the system are made during hardware/software co-design, the driver availability for the OS of our choice is also considered. In certain cases, the device vendor may not have the driver for the OS we want to use. In that case, we might have to either use a different device that provides the same functionality or the device vendor might provide the specification of their device and we might have to write the driver ourselves. It is also possible to influence the device vendor to provide the driver for the OS of our choice; it's a business decision for the device vendor.

3. Sensing, navigation, and control: This is more custom software that we may have to design and develop on our own. There are drone kits available on the market. If we chose to use a particular drone

kit, then this piece is available as part of the kit. However, for a custom solution, we will have write our own sensing, navigation, and control system.

4. Application-specific components: Application-specific components, as the name suggests, are based on the intended usage of the drone. There are plenty of applications we could start with and then customize to meet our purpose.

Logistics and Operations Management

Logistics and operations management is critical to the success of the project, which involves high volume manufacturing. Commercial drones are usually produced in high volumes. Agricultural drones like Crop Squad will be manufactured in lesser volumes, but the process of logistics and operation management will be same when it is built by bigger companies partnering with ODM/OEMs. Logistics and operations management is also referred to as supply chain management, and includes all the operations end to end, from the extraction of raw materials to the manufacturing of the end product. Logistics is the key function in meeting market requirements quickly, flexibly, and without incurring inventory cost. There are representatives from the designers, third-party vendors supplying materials, and the factory to manage the logistics and supply chain.

Operations management tracks the overall project schedule, supply chain, stakeholder management, and coordination of internal teams, third-party vendors, and external customers.

Each party or the company participating in the development of the drone benefits from the success of the product; this is common for all types of products, not just drones.

Board and System Assembly

The supply chain management makes sure that the line items of the system BOM and EBOM will be available on the scheduled date for PCB assembly and system assembly.

Demand BOM

The demand BOM generates reservations for components that are in stock and requisitions for components that are not in stock. Each part has a unique part number. This includes the buy items and make items of the board as well as the system. Buy items are the parts that need to be procured from third-party suppliers; they already have unique manufacturer part numbers. Make items will not have a manufacturer or manufacturer part number because they are custom made in the internal design house.

Production BOM

A production BOM is the final BOM. It is hierarchical in nature and includes all board-level and system-level components, subassemblies, and software required for the final product build.

Exactly two weeks before the PCBA build and system build, the BOM needs to be frozen, after which no parts can be added. The addition of any new component in this phase will cause a delay in the PCBA or product build, which will affect the overall product schedule. Two weeks is not a standard practice; it depends on the lead time of the parts used in the BOM. The lead time of some special parts can be in terms of months. Any part added at the last minute with a month-long lead time will hold the PCBA and system build until that part docks in the factory.

Summary

In this chapter, we quickly skimmed through the overall product system design flow. We also talked about some specific considerations of a drone system. Additionally, we created the high-level definition of the drone system that we plan to design. Overall, the chapter sets the background for the detailed discussion of the drone system design that we will go though in the next chapters.

CHAPTER 3

Key Ingredients and Selection Considerations

In the previous chapter, you saw the drone system design flow, specifically the architecture of the drone with respect to mechanicals, hardware, and software. In this chapter, you'll explore the details of each ingredient and the key considerations when selecting the ingredients via a few examples.

It is always good for a designer to remember the basics while selecting an ingredient. Technology keeps improving day by day. Keeping the fundamentals handy will help designers select components quickly and avoid mistakes.

Detailed study and analysis is important when selecting a component. Unlike software, hardware is one part of the system where no modification or rework can be done after build or manufacturing. Reworks can provide temporary fixes in hardware, but for stable operation and reliability of the hardware, permanent fixes or redesigns are required. To fix the issue, the hardware has to go through the complete development cycle again or with minimal changes in the affected areas. There might be multiple revisions required to perfect the design. These changes may or may not affect the mechanical sections to some extent.

© Neeraj Kumar Singh, Porselvan Muthukrishnan, Satyanarayana Sanpini 2019
N. K. Singh et al., *Industrial System Engineering for Drones*,
https://doi.org/10.1007/978-1-4842-3534-8_3

System on a Chip

Drones, to function properly; they require similar components that we see in robots, smartphones, and wearable smart devices in order to offer different existing applications within drone and any future technology upgrades.

One such critical component is the SoC (system on a chip). This SoC powers most of the current generation's systems such as drones, smartphones, wearables, and appliances. The following is a list of blocks usually integrated inside a sample SoC:

- *CPU*: The central processing unit, usually a single core processor but occasionally multiple core processors.

- *Memory*: Mostly the first-level and second-level cache memories, which are SRAMS, for performing the various tasks of the drone.

- *GPU*: The graphics processing unit is responsible for displaying the output and acceleration in case of high-end games. It may not be required for the drone's applications. Most drones don't use a display.

- *Northbridge*: The interface that handles the communication between the CPU and other components of the SOC and the southbridge.

- *Southbridge*: A companion chip for the CPU inside the SOC that handles all of the IO functions.

- *DSP*: Digital signal processors for analog and audio applications inside the SOC.

- *WiFi and cellular radios*: Some SOCs integrate digital parts of components like WiFi+BT modems and 3G/4G cellular modems GPS for direct wireless connectivity.

The technical specifications of the SOC depend entirely on the intended application. SOC specs such as processing speed and memory capacity are different for different applications. For example, an agricultural drone meant to perform crop monitoring will do more tasks within the subsystems or the peripherals than the processors. The critical subsystems are overloaded than the processors in a crop monitoring drone, which is explained in detail below.

- *Cameras*: Continuously capture still images or videos of the target crops.

- *ISPs*: Image signal processors convert the raw capture to a specific format that a computer can read or the software application can recognize for further processing. video compression is done in the ISPs if the data is large and needs to be uploaded through the network.

- *Network modem*: Establishes the connection between the drone and the IP network/Cloud/server and helps to upload the enormous data for further processing if required.

Most of the latest generation SOCs integrate ISPs. In such case, the ISPs inside the SOC get the raw capture from the camera though a direct digital interface without any compression, apply the required image or video processing algorithms, and compress the data before converting it into any standard file format.

Categories

There are always multiple choices when selecting the SoC for a drone, like any other electronic products. There are specific features to be looked at when selecting the SOC for a drone. Additionally, there are power, performance, and memory requirements. There are two major categories of SoCs preferred these days: x86 and ARM.

Key Considerations

The following list of processor characteristics covers the key considerations for selecting an SOC:

1. Core count

2. Core frequency

3. Cache memory

4. Primary memory controller

5. Subsystem interfaces

6. Power consumption

The core count, frequency, cache, and memory considerations depend on the workload (application) of the drone. Obviously, more cores with large cache memory will perform better than a single core with lesser cache memory. The higher the frequency, the higher the performance by any processor because it executes more instructions per second. However, if the workload is such that it does not leverage the higher core count (via parallelism), then there is no point in selecting a multicore processor.

Solutions

Designer can choose any processor for the drone from the different variants available. For example, there is wide range of processors available from the Intel x86 architecture.

A drone, especially a crop monitoring drone equipped with high-performance hyperspectral camera, needs more memory, integrated image processing, and high-speed interfaces like USB 3.1 and PCIe for the camera interface.

The other blocks of the SOC can be minimal and sufficient if they meet the basic requirements.

Memory

There are different layers of memory systems. The first layer (L1) and second layer (L2) memories reside on the CPU or SOC. They're called the cache memory and are usually static random-access memory (SRAM). The next layer of memory present externally is the primary memory of the system, which is usually dynamic random-access memory (DRAM). SRAM and DRAM are volatile storage devices.

In modern computer systems, many types of memory devices are available. Primary memories can be either volatile, non-volatile, or hybrid. The most widely used primary memories are DDR SDRAM (double data rate – synchronous dynamic random-access memory). Selecting the right memory for any electronic system is a big task.

In late 1996, SDRAM began to appear in systems. Unlike previous technologies, SDRAM is designed to synchronize itself with the timing of the CPU. This enables the memory controller to know the exact clock cycle when the requested data will be ready, so the CPU no longer has to wait between memory accesses. SDRAM can stand for SDR SDRAM (single data rate SDRAM), where the I/O, internal clock, and bus clock are the same.

DDR-SDRAM achieves greater bandwidth by transferring data on the rising and falling edges of the clock signal. It doubles the transfer rate without increasing the frequency of the clock.

Categories

In a system, the basic operating system loads the primary memory; on top of that, additional memory space is required to load other applications. There are different types of DRAM available on the market.

Standard DRAM

Detailed analysis is required to select the right memory device for the system.

First Generation

The next generation of SDRAM is DDR, which achieves greater bandwidth than the preceding single data rate SDRAM by transferring data on the rising and falling edges of the clock signal (double pumped). Effectively, it doubles the transfer rate without increasing the frequency of the clock. The transfer rate of DDR SDRAM is the double of SDR SDRAM without changing the internal clock. In DDR SDRAM, as the first generation of DDR memory, the prefetch buffer is 2 bits, which is double of SDR SDRAM. The transfer rate of DDR is between 266~400 MT/s. DDR266 and DDR400 are of this type.

Second Generation

Its primary benefit is the ability to operate the external data bus twice as fast as DDR SDRAM. This is achieved by an improved bus signal. The prefetch buffer of DDR2 is 4 bits (double of DDR SDRAM). DDR2 memory is at the same internal clock speed (133~200MHz) as DDR, but the transfer rate of DDR2 can reach 533~800 MT/s with the improved I/O bus signal. DDR2 533 and DDR2 800 memory types are on the market.

Third Generation

DDR3 memory offers 40% less power consumption compared to current DDR2 modules, allowing for lower operating currents and voltages (1.5 V, compared to DDR2's 1.8 V or DDR's 2.5 V). The transfer rate of DDR3 is 800~1600 MT/s. DDR3's prefetch buffer width is 8 bits, whereas DDR2's is 4 bits, and DDR's is 2 bits. DDR3 also adds two functions: ASR (automatic self-refresh) and SRT (self-refresh temperature). They can make the memory control the refresh rate according to the temperature variation.

Fourth Generation

DDR4 SDRAM provides a lower operating voltage (1.2V) and higher transfer rate. The transfer rate of DDR4 is 2133~3200 MT/s. DDR4 adds four new bank groups technology. Each bank group has the feature of singlehanded operation. DDR4 can process four data within a clock cycle, so DDR4's efficiency is better than DDR3 obviously. DDR4 also adds some functions, such as DBI (data bus inversion), CRC (cyclic redundancy check), and CA parity. They can enhance DDR4 memory's signal integrity and improve the stability of data transmission/access.

Fifth Generation

DDR5 SDRAM, in computing interface development, is the abbreviation for the fifth generation of double data rate synchronous dynamic random-access memory. DDR5 is planned to reduce power consumption once again, while doubling bandwidth and capacity relative to DDR4 SDRAM.

Mobile DRAM

The standard DRAM made for computers uses too much power, so companies developed more power-efficient mobile DRAM for the growing market of smart gadgets. Mobile DRAM works in same way as standard DRAM but differs in size, heat, and power consumption. Mobile DRAM is also called as low-power double data rate memory (LPDDR).

All LPDDR memory operates at low voltage (1.8, 1.2 volts), unlike the traditional voltages of corresponding standard DDR (2.5, 1.8 volts). All other parameters are similar to standard DDR memory, other than the power supply.

In a mobile DRAM device, address control and command are shared between the devices.

Key Considerations

The selection of the memory device is based on the system software requirements and also depends on the SOC. 2GB is the minimum required memory to run a basic Windows/Linux OS, but 8GB might be used in some systems to execute additional applications, heavy graphics, or additional acceleration. This drone OS and system software may not require 8GB, because neither it needs to run complex applications nor any heavy graphics and the overall system is not that complicated. Only few applications will be running on the base OS of the drone. For illustration purpose, let's assume 8GB is the requirement, as shown in the architecture diagram. So we need to find a device with the following parameters:

- Technology supported on the SOC

- Memory capacity or density supported on the SOC

- Data bus width of memory controller on the SOC

- Memory controller operating the frequency/clock rate

- Data rate

- Operating temperature of the system

- Package size

If the memory controller of the SOC doesn't support 8GB memory, then there is no way the system can have 8GB. Either the system requirements or the SOC must change.

Data bus width determines the memory rank and number of devices. A memory rank is a set of DRAM chips connected to the same chip select, which are therefore accessed simultaneously.

Solutions

Memory technology is always evolving. The most commonly used memory devices at present in maximum electronic gadgets are standard DDR3 or LPDDR3. DDR4 and LPDDR4 are already on the market and are penetrating gadgets at a fast pace. DDR5 and LPDDR5 are still in development stages. LPDDR3 solution below is the cheapest and matured solution for a drone which is explained below.

If only one controller with a 64-bit bus width is available in the SOC, and the maximum density available in a single device is 32 Gb (equivalent to 4GB) with a 64-bit bus width from a particular vendor, two of these devices are required for 8GB memory.

So two 32 Gb devices are selected for the drone. The memory solution for the drone with the 8GB requirement is shown in Figure 3-1.

Since the SOC has a 64-bit width data bus, which is split into two 32-bit width data buses to each of the devices, address command and control (clock enable, chip select, and on die termination signals) signals are common to both devices.

There are only two device loads; the single clock signal is provided for both the devices as a tree connection. If there are more than two loads, two individual clocks must drive each memory device pair (for a total of four devices). These clock and data signals are high-speed signals operating in GHz, so the signal routing should follow strict electrical guidelines to avoid degradation and for better functionality and performance. This will ensure the stable operation of the memory in a system even in at full load and prolonged operation (stress test).

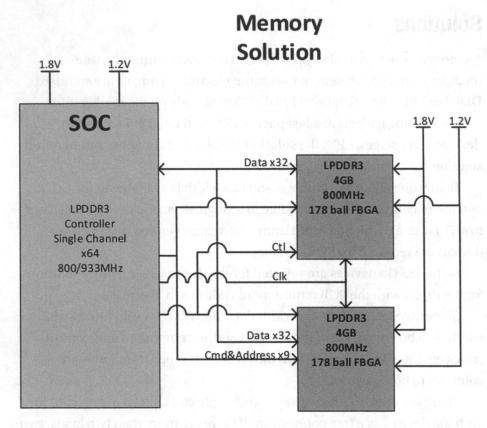

Figure 3-1. Memory solution block diagram

Apart from the design, the device also should meet other electrical and mechanical requirements of the intended system. For example, a drone design may allow less space to accommodate the PCB, due to its complicated structure with multiple discrete mechanical elements. To achieve the smallest PCB, finding a smaller memory package is necessary, and this will reduce the overall board size. Similarly, the device has to meet other criteria specific for a drone applications. A crop monitoring drone is a outdoor device, may need industrial grade temperature, which is -40 to +85°C.

The following is the list of key features of the selected device. All of the parameters and corresponding values given in the datasheets must meet the system requirements.

- Frequency range of 800/933 MHz (data rate: 1600/1866 Mb/s/pin)

- Lead-free (RoHS-compliant) and halogen-free packaging

- VDD1/VDD2/VDDCA/VDDQ: 1.8V/1.2V/1.2V/1.2V

- Array configuration

  - 128MB x 64 (DDP)

  - 256MB x 64 (QDP)

- Packaging

  - 12.0mm X 11.5mm, 178-ball FBGA package

  - 13.0mm X 11.5mm, 178-ball FBGA package

- Operating temperature from -30°C to +85°C

Storage

Every system needs a storage device, which is a nonvolatile memory to store the application and data. This secondary storage can be either internal or external to the system. The operating system resides on this secondary storage in any typical computer or electronic gadget. It also serves as permanent storage for other files, like documents and video.

Categories

There are different types of storage devices based on the different technologies that have evolved over the years. Some are outdated, and others get improved every day.

Magnetic Storage

Floppy disks and hard disk drives are the major magnetic storage devices on the digital computer. Floppy disks are not used anymore. Hard disks are large and heavy and are not suitable for currently generation electronic devices, wearables or drones.

Figure 3-2 shows a hard disk drive and a floppy disk, which are typical magnetic storage devices.

Desktops use 3.5-inch hard disks while laptops use 2.5-inch hard disks. Both form factors are too big to use for any small form factory designs like drones and wearables.

Figure 3-2. *Magnetic storage devices*

Optical Storage

Optical storage consists of the devices that store data on optical disks. Data is stored or read with the aid of a beam from a laser. Compact disks (CDs), digital versatile disks (DVDs), and Blue Ray disks are still in use today. The size and shape are similar to hard disk drives. However, these drives can't be accommodated in drone designs or gadgets as secondary storage device.

In a desktop computer, the standard optical drive comes in a 5.25-inch form factor. These disk drives are connected to the motherboard via a standard cable. A typical example of an optical disk drive along with a Blue Ray storage disk placed on a tray is shown in Figure 3-3.

Figure 3-3. *Optical drive and disk*

Flash Storage

Flash memory is the type of storage device widely used on embedded systems and gadgets. Flash storage is a semiconductor-based different form of solid state storage device. The advantages of flash storage over magnetic and optical storage devices are

- Flash storage is very compact.

- It is mechanically more stable and resistant to mechanical movements.

- Very low power consumption.

- Internal or external to the system.

- Low cost.

The two main types of flash storage devices are NOR and NAND. The parameters are shown in Table 3-1.

Table 3-1. *NOR vs. NAND Flash*

Parameter	NOR	NAND
Read speed	Fast	Slow
Write speed	Slow	Fast
Erase time	Fast	Slow
Addressing	Memory mapped address	By row and column address
Direct read	Yes	No
Error detection and correction	No	Yes
Application	Program/mass storage	Program

Both NAND and NOR flash devices are used as secondary memories in systems in different forms of solid state storage. They can be either internal, a device soldered on the board, or external through a JEDEC standard connector.

CompactFlash

CompactFlash is a popular external memory used in cameras and other handheld devices that need large storage. Based on the Parallel Advanced Technology Attached interface, CF cards measure 43.8mm by 36.4mm and are available with storage capacities ranging up to 512 GB. Though this is smaller than a magnetic device, it's still too big for a consumer drone.

CompactFlash cards need 3.3V or 5V for operation. CompactFlash memory is usually an external storage device. A standard CompactFlash connector is present on the system where the flash device will be plugged in. Figure 3-4 shows a typical compact storage device.

Figure 3-4. *CompactFlash storage*

Multimedia Card

A multimedia card (MMC) is a NOR-flash-based low-pin-count serial interface memory. MMC cards measure 24mm X 32mm X 1.4mm. MMC cards are available with storage capacities up to 512 GB.

MMC needs 3.3V for operation. Similar to CompactFlash, MMC are plugged into a connector on the system's side.

If the system needs the MMC storage without the external connector, there is another version called embedded multimedia controller (eMMC). eMMC is an IC package consisting of both flash memory and a flash memory controller integrated on the same silicon die.

The package size is a standard 11.5mm x 13mm X 1.0mm 153 pin BGA device. eMMCs occupy less space on the board with minimal external components. Figure 3-5 shows a typical MMC card. This BGA package version of MMC may be a perfect fit for a drone design.

Figure 3-5. *MMC/SD card*

Secure Digital Card

Secure Digital (SD) is another NAND flash-based low-pin-count serial interface memory, similar to a MMC card but with improvements. There are different versions of SD cards available in various speeds and voltage levels.

Unlike CompactFlash and MMC, SD cards support different sizes: standard, mini, and micro. These three physical sizes make the SD card a more convenient choice for most current generation systems.

- Standard size:

    - SD (SDSC), SDHC, SDXC, SDIO

    - 32.0x24.0x2.1mm

    - 32.0x24.0x1.4mm

- Mini size:

    - SD, SDHC, SDIO

    - 21.5x20.0x1.4mm

- Micro size:

  - SD, SDHC, SDXC

  - 15.0x11.0x1.0mm

Figure 3-6 shows a typical micro SD card. It may be the perfect fit for the drone's external expandable storage.

Figure 3-6. *Micro SD card*

Solid State Drives

Flash-based SSDs are storage devices that primarily use electronics interfaces compatible with traditional block input/output hard disk drives. The SSD form factor is the same as that of a traditional hard disk drive.

Unlike hard disk drives, SSDs have no mechanical components. SSDs are more resistant to physical shocks than other flash storage devices. SSD uses NAND flash technology.

There is other version of SSD available: micro SSD. It can be soldered on the board with the interfaces directly connecting to the SOC instead of using a bulky connector. This device package is also small and best suited for a smaller form factor design like drones. However, it's an expensive solution compared to all other storage technologies.

Figure 3-7 shows a typical example of a SSD drive. This is a connector-based SSD solution with a form factor similar to a SATA hard drive.

Figure 3-7. *SSD drive*

USB Flash Storage

A USB flash drive is a data storage device that includes flash memory with an integrated USB interface. Figure 3-8 shows the typical example of a USB memory stick. USB memory is basic requirement for embedded systems or wearables. Micro and mini USB connectors are also available to reduce the footprint of the connector on the board. The latest development in the USB standard is the Type C connector (USB 3 and USB 4), which supports high-speed storage in a smaller form factor.

Figure 3-8. *USB memory stick*

Key Considerations

A drone system will always be exposed to mechanical stresses like vibrations, free fall, and drops. It is better to avoid storage devices with mechanical parts. This clearly eliminates the mechanical and optical storage devices as secondary storage devices for drones. Also, drone designs should avoid storage devices with connectors. Storage devices soldered down on the board are ideal.

Which means, the integrated eMMC and uSSD devices are the most suitable for drones. The storage capacity of eMMC and uSSD are limited. The current technology doesn't support capacity beyond 256GB per device. Terabyte eMMC and uSSD may be available in the future. For uSSD, a standard SATA interface is required from the host side, which offers lower pin count compared to the eMMC and SD card interfaces.

The micro SD card (SDXC) format can go up to terabytes, which also occupies less space on the board with a higher pin count compared to uSSD.

Considering all the parameters, uSSD looks to be a better solution, though it is expensive than the others. The higher the capacity, the higher the price for any flash device.

Generally, no system depends on a single storage device. The same rule applies for drones. If the space is available, providing additional backup storage devices is necessary. If uSSD serves as the principal integrated memory, SD card and USB flash devices can serve as external extended storage devices. The system has to accommodate SD card and USB connectors to enable the backup storage. These storage devices can be plugged into the system when required.

The following is the list of key parameters to be checked before selecting a storage device:

- Storage capacity

- Size

- Cost

- Host interface
- Operating voltage
- Security features like encryption and authentication

Solutions

Micro SSD is perfect for very small factor devices like drones and other embedded systems. The micro SSD BGA package combines a SATA flash controller with the latest in small geometry SLC NAND flash, multiple power supplies, and security features including encryption, authentication, RNG, anti-tamper, and a self-destruct feature in a single device. For illustration purpose, the device selected for the drone has the following features:

- Host accessible capacity up to 128GB
- Integrated switching power supplies with a single power supply 3.3V
- Footprint replaceable with 256GB and higher-capacity devices
- Zero power standby
- 524-pin BGA package of 32mm X 28mm

In addition to the micro SSD part, a micro SD card connector or a USB connector can be provided on the system for the external detachable storage devices. There can be multiple storage solutions for any systems for backup if the PCB has the available space to accommodate these devices. The storage solution for the drone is shown in Figure 3-9.

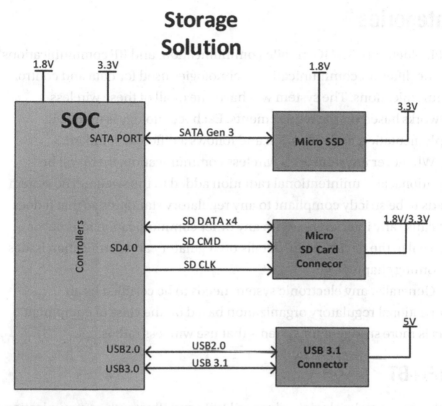

Figure 3-9. *Storage solution for the drone*

Communication Module

The communication module is the device capable of transmitting analog or digital signals over a wired or wireless communication channel. The module interfaces with the host processor through any of the standard interfaces like UART, SDIO, or PCIe. The digital data from the host processors is converted to a protocol suitable for modulation/demodulation and then transmitted through wireless protocols. There are different categories of wireless networks, based on the speed, distance, and data rate requirements of the system. The higher the performance, the higher the implementation cost of the wireless networks.

Categories

WiFi, Bluetooth, 3G/4G mobile communication, and RF communications are the different communication technologies used for data and control communications. The system will have one or all of these wireless networks based on the requirements. Each technology is unique in implementation and operation and follows a different standard.

Whenever a system adds wireless communication, there will be intentional and unintentional radiation added to the system. The system needs to be strictly compliant to any regulatory standards so that it does not cause any interference with any other communication internal or external to the device. More details on regulatory and certification issues in upcoming chapters.

Generally, any electronic system needs to be certified by an international regulatory organization based on the class of equipment. This is more stringent for systems that use wireless radios.

WiFi+BT

With current technologies, advanced WiFi and Bluetooth communication technologies are integrated. These compact short-range modules are fully certified with integrated antennas and software stacks that can interface with the SOC with a simple UART interface. There are some more advanced modules available with the PCIe interface to achieve a very high data rate.

These modules can be placed on the board (PCB antenna) and expose the integrated antenna without any external antenna by covering it with nonmetallic mechanical parts. These modules are available in different form factors and are easy to integrate and plug-and-play with the host processor. Pre-certified M.2, MiniPCIe, and LGA module packages are a few of the standard packaging available.

All the WiFi devices are based on the IEEE 802.11 standard. Wi-Fi is a trademark of the Wi-Fi Alliance, which restricts the use of the term "Wi-Fi Certified" to products that successfully complete interoperability certification testing. Figure 3-10 shows an M.2 form factor WiFi+BT module that can be plugged into the drone system. The connector for this module is part of the primary motherboard of the drone.

Figure 3-10. *Integrated WIFI+BT module in a M.2 form factor*

Mobile Network

Adding a mobile network to the drone provides many advantages. Mobile connectivity primarily helps the drone for command and control. This also improves safety because all the real-time information from the drone can be sent over the network to the drone traffic management. A mobile network on the drone also helps control drone beyond the line of sight, provided the area has enough network coverage.

The different types of mobile networks that can be added to the drone are 3G, 4G (LTE), or the current 5G network. Similar to the WiFi+BT module, precertified cellular modems are available from different wireless companies. These modems are available in different categories for different bands corresponding to different regions.

Long-Term Evolution (LTE) is the current high-speed mobile network used extensively. LTE is a high-speed wireless communication based on its predecessors, the GSM/EDGE and UMTS/HSPA technologies. It increases the capacity and speed using a different radio interface together with core network improvements. LTE devices are based on the 3GPP standard.

IR/RF Wireless

Many drones, embedded systems, wearables, and appliances have IR or RF remote controls. These days, commercial, off-the-shelf RF transmitters and receivers are available for drones. The off-the-shelf transmitter-receiver combination can be used to control the drones remotely and to stream video and audio remotely. Miniature modules are available with the latest technology and can be directly integrated with the system.

Several 2.4 GHz precertified solutions are readily available. Modern 2.4GHz RF protocols have higher bandwidth data rates and can allow audio and video streams independent of control links.

Key Considerations

A wireless connection is mandatory to control the drone remotely. There are different ways of implementing the control links and data links for the drone system. In a crop monitoring drone, there can be a single solution for control and data communication or there can be two dedicated channels for control and data communication.

The coverage area for a wireless LAN and a mobile network is limited, so the drone needs a RF communication channel for a control link to cover longer distances.

RF remote control can be the dedicated control path, and WiFi+BT or mobile network can be the dedicated data path. Considering that the drone needs to live stream the data or access the cloud for analysis at regular intervals, either the wireless LAN or the mobile network will serve the purpose.

WiFi+BT is a better solution than a mobile network in terms of cost, power consumption, and design complexity. Live streaming of data is not possible if the drone is not in the network coverage area. The drone needs to process the data offline or fly to the coverage area to upload data. Another way is to add more WiFi access points near the drone's fly zone.

Solution

The wireless solutions for drones vary in technology, size, and cost. The basic features of the WiFi+BT solution of Intel-based module are shown in Figure 3-11 and listed below. The solution is the designer's choice based on the application of the drone.

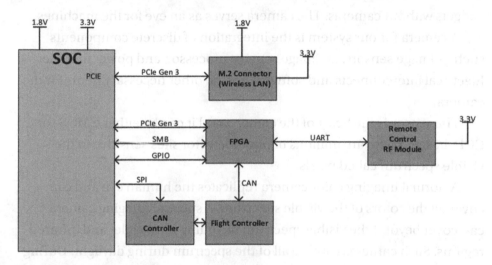

Figure 3-11. *Drone communication solution*

The WiFi module selected is the M.2 form factor pluggable precertified module. The features of the module are as follows:

- Dual-band wireless AC: 2.4 GHz, 5 GHz

- TX/RX streams: 1X1

- Max speed: 433 Mbps

- WiFi Certified: 802.11ac

- Bluetooth version: 4.2

- Size: 22mm X 30mm X 2.4mm

- Host interface: PCIe, USB

- Form factor: M.2 2230, 1216

Camera

Cameras play a significant role in systems that offer imaging as a primary function. These days, it's very difficult to find electronics systems or gadgets without cameras. The camera serves as an eye for the machines.

A camera for our system is the integration of discrete components such as image sensors, an image sensing processor, and power modules. Electrical interconnects and software are the other necessary items for the camera.

The sensor is the heart of the camera, and it can be either CMOS- or CCD-based. There are millions of photodetector sites sensitive to the visible spectrum called pixels.

A normal imaging color camera replicates the human eye and can cover all the colors of the visible spectrum. A spectral imaging camera can cover beyond the visible spectrum including ultra violet and infrared regions. Such cameras capture all of the spectrum during daylight. During the absence of sunlight, the target objects should be illuminated with high temperature (around 3000K) halogen lamps to capture the infrared spectrum.

Categories

Every digital camera sensor works by capturing light in an array of photo sites. When the exposure begins, each side is uncovered by shutters to collect the incoming light. When the shutter closes, the exposure ends and the content of each photo site is read as an electrical signal, which is stored as a numerical value in an image file. The stored values measure the quantity of light.

The camera module usually supports the USB 2, MIPI, and LVDS interfaces. The latest and most advanced camera modules support the USB 3.1 host interface. This makes system integration easier with the module.

Monochrome

Monochrome sensors capture all of the incoming light at each pixel, regardless of color. Each pixel captures 3x more light, since red, green, and blue are absorbed. Monochrome sensors are able to capture higher resolution images.

Color

Color sensors capture only one of the three primary colors at each photo site in an alternating pattern, using something called a color filter array. The most successful is the Bayer Pattern, which uses alternating rows of red-green and green-blue filters.

Unlike with monochrome, each pixel effectively captures 1/3 of the incoming light, since any color not matching the pattern is filtered out. Any red or blue light that hits a green pixel won't be recorded.

Spectral Imaging

Spectral imaging, also known as hyperspectral imaging, provides a digital image with far more spectral information for each pixel than traditional color images. The raw capture has a stack of tens to hundreds of pictures with each successive image representing its own specific color, or equivalently, as a detailed spectral curve for each pixel.

Key Considerations

For a crop monitoring drone, a simple monochrome or color cameras will not suffice. The camera has to go beyond the color wavelengths to capture the anatomy of leaves, stem, pods, flowers, and fruits. For example, to monitor leaf health and nutrition value, the camera has to capture the internal chlorophyll pattern and distribution, which is beyond the visible spectrum and includes the IR and UV region.

The system can have multiple cameras to cover the intended spectrum. The system can combine a primary hyperspectral camera and additional monochrome or color cameras to improve the accuracy of the system.

In a drone system, the camera module needs to be placed externally or protrude on the bottom with rotatable plate, so that it covers 360-degree field of view. These modules can be off the shelf or custom-made as per the system requirement.

The power source and host interface can be through the external UBS 3.0 cable from the module to the system or through a separate power cable in addition to the USB 3.0 data cable.

Solutions

A single hyperspectral imaging camera is mandatory for a crop monitoring drone. There can be other cameras like a flight view or a first person view camera for a better user control experience. Users can observe the flight path in a display attached to the remote control.

The imaging solution for our hyperspectral crop monitoring drone is shown in Figure 3-12.

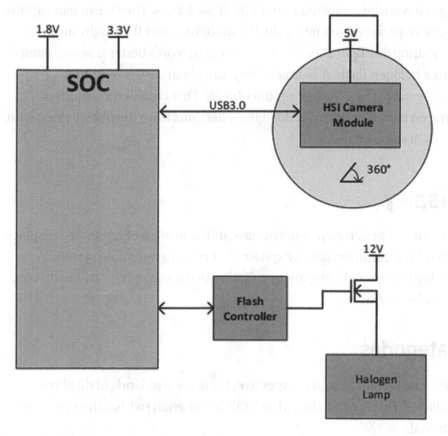

Figure 3-12. *Drone imaging solution*

The features of the hyperspectral imaging camera module are as follows:

- Sensor: Hyperspectral imaging

- Type: Line scan

- Spectral range: 600-970

- Bands: 100+

- Host interface: USB 3.0

A hyperspectral imaging sensor can generate a RGB color image aligned with spectral images with multiple bands. The sensor can capture all the required wavelengths during daylight under the bright sunlight.

During low light conditions, the camera works better if accompanied with a halogen flash. A halogen lamp can generate the required temperature when flashed on the objects. This creates the required infrared wavelengths from the light reflections from the object along with the RGB color image.

Display

The current generation systems have different sizes of integrated displays. A display is required for any system that runs an operating system. A display is helpful during the installation of the operating system, drivers, and other software.

Categories

From the system design perspective, there are two kinds of displays available. Displays can be either built-in (internal) within the system or external.

Internal

Internal displays are commonly used in laptops, tablets, and mobile phones. An internal display makes the device more portable and reduces the dependencies from external displays for development, operation, debugging, and troubleshooting of the system. Since they must be built into a system that is already small, the display must be smaller with less resolution. Smaller displays can offer an integrated touch screen, which is a more convenient input device these days.

Internal displays are powered using internally generated power from the system. The backlight used for the display will be the most power-consuming subsystem.

Generally, the host interface used in internal displays is LVDS, MIPI, or eDP. The displays either integrate the controller inside or externally. Even if there is no compatible interface in the SOC, there are options available to convert any display, interface, and protocol to make it compatible for the display.

External

External displays are standard computer monitors available in various sizes and a wide range of resolutions. These displays are powered externally and connect to the system either by a standard AV cable, a VGA cable, a DVI cable, or HDMI cable.

External displays are more suitable for the system, which doesn't need a monitor all the time. It's only required when there is a system upgrade, installation, development, debugging, or any other activity. However, a display is not mandatory for any embedded system.

Key Considerations

A display is not mandatory for the drone system. An external display connector can be added as a backup display. An optional display can be added on the remote controller to get a first person view of the drone during the flight. This gives a better user experience for the operators.

An external display can be any of the low profile display connectors like micro HDMI, mini DP, or Type C. This will help check and analyze the images from the drone directly by connecting a monitor externally when the drone is not in flight.

An optional integrated display can be attached to the remote controller. A dedicated video transfer communication channel is required between the drone and the remote to live stream the video.

Flight Controllers

The flight controller is the most important subsystem in a drone. A flight controller receives commands from the user and controls the propellers and motors to keep the drone in flight. It also receives other commands like image capture, video capture, and any other use case commands from the user and executes them while the drone is in the air.

Categories

There are different types of off-the-shelf flight controllers readily available specifically for drones. They are available in different form factors and varying sizes.

MCU/MPU

Microcontroller/microprocessor-based flight controllers are available in different form factors. They are plug-and-play and can be integrated with the system with less effort. The performance of the controllers and the accuracy of the sensors will vary with the cost. Obviously, high performance flight controllers are more expensive.

FPGA

Other than microcontrollers and microprocessors, there are FPGA or custom-made ASIC-based high performance flight controllers available. They are the most expensive solutions that integrate additional capability. A system that doesn't need an off-the-shelf flight controller can have an on-board FPGA with on-board sensors.

Key Considerations

Key considerations for a flight controller are the complexity of integration with the system, supported sensors, flying capability, and cost. Most advanced flight controllers are easy to install and integrate with the host computer.

Solutions

The features of any flight controller are listed as follows in the product brief or in the datasheet:

- 32-bit microcontroller/ARM cortex processor/FPGA
- Gyroscope and accelerometers
- Barometer
- Magnetometer
- GPS
- Supports quadcopter, hexcopter, tricopter, and octocopter

Battery

Drones are supposed to fly high, so they must carry their own power supply. Drones are powered using fuel, solar, or batteries. For industrial drones used in the agriculture field, the battery is the main source of the power. The battery is recharged when the drone is not in use or is stationed.

Categories

Most electronics gadgets and drones these days use rechargeable batteries. The most common rechargeable batteries are covered in the following sections.

Lead Acid

Lead acid is the oldest rechargeable battery system. Lead acid is rugged, forgiving if abused, and economically priced. But it has a low specific energy and limited cycle count. Lead acid is used for wheelchairs, golf cars, personnel carriers, emergency lighting, and uninterruptible power supplies.

Nickel Cadmium

Mature and well understood, NiCd is used where long service life, high discharge current, and extreme temperatures are required. NiCd is one of the most rugged and enduring batteries; it is the only chemistry that allows ultra-fast charging with minimal stress. Its main applications are power tools, medical devices, aviation, and UPS. Due to environmental concerns, NiCd is being replaced with other chemistries, but it retains its status in aircrafts due to its good safety record.

Nickel Metal Hydride

NiMH serves as a replacement for NiCd as it has only mild toxic metals and provides higher specific energy. NiMH is used for medical instruments, hybrid cars, and industrial applications. NiMH is also available in AA and AAA cells for consumer use.

Lithium-Ion Batteries

Li-ion is taking over many applications that were previously served by lead and nickel-based batteries. Due to safety concerns, Li-ion needs a protection circuit. It is more expensive than most other batteries, but its high cycle count and low maintenance reduce the cost per cycle over many other chemistries.

Lithium batteries are the most suitable batteries in electronic gadgets and especially in drones based on the following features and advantages:

- Characteristics: Small dry cell batteries, sealed, rechargeable

- Form factor: Custom sizes in plastic cases, small cylinders, button cells

- Applications: Cell phones, laptops, power tools, hybrid automobiles, video cameras, handheld electronics, drones

- Safety: Non-spillable, non-toxic

Key Considerations

The first step in any battery selection is calculating the max current consumption of the drone system. System power consumption varies based on the KPIs. Maximum power is drawn during the max KPI, which drains the battery at a faster rate.

For example, if the drone power consumption is 10A during the video recording in flight, a 10000mA battery will last for an hour.

The nominal voltage of the battery is based on the battery architecture. If a single cell of a lithium ion battery can generate nominal 3.7V, 10A, two such cells in parallel will generate same voltage with twice the current, so 20A. Two such cells in series will generate twice the amount of voltage 7.2

with 10A of current. So for a drone, the cell architecture should be two cells in a series, which is also called 2S1P architecture, which means two cells in series and one parallel.

There is another parameter called charge rate on the datasheet. Usually the charger design is based on the standard charging rate. However, some systems need fast charging to reduce the charging time of the system. In that case, the charger design should be done in such a way as to charge the batteries at the faster rates.

Solutions

Battery specifications are generally listed in the vendor datasheets and are as follows:

- Nominal capacity: 10000mAh

- Nominal voltage: 7.2V

- Voltage at end of discharge: 5.6V

- Charging voltage: 8.56V

- Standard charge: 0.2C CC/CV

- Standard discharge: 0.2C CC/CV

- Fast charge: 0.5C CC/CV

- Fast discharge: 0.5C CC

- Maximum continuous charge current: 5000mA

- Maximum continuous discharge current: 5000mA

- Product dimension: Length x width x thickness in mm

Thermal Solution

A common problem in product design, particularly in electronics, is managing the thermal conditions for optimal efficiency. The core of the challenge is designing energy-efficient microprocessors and printed circuit boards that will not overheat.

A frequently overlooked aspect of thermal management problem solving is architectural design. Whether it's a private home, an office building, or a dedicated server room or drone, architectural considerations can have a huge impact on the thermal management solutions available.

Categories

To tackle and alleviate the difficulties and inefficiencies that arise as a result of heat, engineers employ different cooling systems to manage conditions. These systems can be divided into two main categories: those with active and those with passive cooling techniques.

Active Cooling

Active cooling refers to cooling technologies that rely on an external device to enhance heat transfer. Through active cooling technologies, the rate of fluid flow increases during convection, which dramatically increases the rate of heat removal.

Active cooling solutions include forced air through a fan or blower, forced liquid, and thermoelectric coolers (TECs), which can be used to optimize thermal management on all levels. Fans are used when natural convection is insufficient to remove heat. They are commonly integrated into electronics, such as computer cases, or are attached to CPUs, hard drives, or chipsets to maintain thermal conditions and reduce failure risk.

The main disadvantage of active thermal management is that it requires the use of electricity and therefore results in higher costs compared to passive cooling.

Passive Cooling

The advantages of passive cooling techniques lie in the energy efficiency and lower financial cost, making it an astute system design choice for the thermal management of both buildings and electronic products.

Passive cooling achieves high levels of natural convection and heat dissipation by utilizing a heat spreader or a heat sink to maximize the radiation and convection heat transfer modes. In architectural design, natural resources like wind or soil are used as heat sinks to absorb or dissipate heat. This leads to proper cooling of electronic products and thermal comfort in homes or office buildings by keeping them under the maximum allowed operating temperature. A growing trend in this regard can be witnessed in what is commonly known in the industry as passive houses.

Passive thermal management is a cost-effective and energy-efficient solution that relies on heat sinks, heat spreaders, heat pipes, or thermal interface materials to maintain optimal operating temperatures.

Key Considerations

Like other electronic gadgets, the boards on drones do need cooling solutions. There are significant advantages and disadvantages of both active and passive cooling systems. There is no restriction on using active or passive. Table 3-2 shows the list of key features to be checked before finalizing a solution.

Table 3-2. *Active vs. Passive Cooling*

Key Features	Active	Passive
Weight	Low	High
Compact size	Yes	No
Noise	Yes	No
Power dissipation	High	Low
Performance degradation	No	Yes
Operation cost	High	Low
Orientation	Yes	No
Reliability	No	High
Eco-friendliness	No	Yes

Solutions

For a drone design, the weight and size of the solution is a high priority. An active cooling solution is the right choice.

Power dissipation is managed by a section of low power fans. Since the drone will be flying to perform the intended application and producing enough noise with the propellers of the quadcopter, noise from the board doesn't make any difference.

A better cooling solution can be provided with active cooling system on a drone system design.

Interconnects

An interconnect is an electrical or optical connection or cable that connects two devices or more. An interconnect joins electric conductors electrically and mechanically to other conductors and to the terminals of electrical devices. Interconnects are passive electrical components that contain two terminals that store energy in their magnetic field, such as a cable connecting a hard drive or a monitor connecting to a computer. A PC contains several interconnects.

Since a drone is a complex electromechanical system, choosing the right interconnects is critical to achieve the best performance.

Categories

There are wide range of interconnect parts from several manufacturers that can be used onboard to connect electrical parts and subsystems. Electronic cable connectors, board-to-board connectors, electrical wire-to-board connectors, RF connectors, and FPC/FFC connectors are the most frequently used connectors for electrical connections on board.

Cable Connectors

USB

The USB connection is quite possibly the most pervasive connection type in today's world. Nearly every form of computer peripheral device like keyboards, mice, headsets, flash drives, and wireless adapters can be connected to your computer through a USB port. The design has evolved over the years, which means there are multiple versions of USB available:

- USB 1.0/1.1 can transmit data at speeds up to 12 Mbps.

- USB 2.0 can transmit data at speeds up to 480 Mbps and is compatible with older versions of USB. At the time of this article, USB 2.0 is the most common type found in the market.

- USB 3.0 can transmit data at speeds up to 4.8 Gbps. It is compatible with previous versions of USB.

The mini and micro USB variants are most often used with smaller, portable devices like PDAs, phones, and digital cameras. The standard USB connectors are more often used on devices that tend to remain plugged in, like external hard drives, keyboards, and mice.

Ethernet

Ethernet cables are used to set up local area networks. In most cases, they're used to connect routers to modems and computers. If you've ever tried to install or fix a home router, you've likely dealt with an Ethernet computer cable. Nowadays, they come in three varieties:

- Cat 5 cables are the most basic type and provide speeds of either 10 Mbps or 100 Mbps.

- Cat 5e, which means Cat 5 Enhanced, allows for faster data transmission than its predecessor. It caps at 1,000 Mbps.

- Cat 6 is the latest and offers the best performance of the three. It's capable of supporting 10 Gbps speeds.

Other than USB and Ethernet, there are different standard cables and cable connectors are available. These cables are categorized into power, data, display, analog, digital, RF cables. VGA, HDMI and DVI are examples for display cables. USB, Ethernet Copper and Ethernet Fiber are examples for data cables.

Board-to-Board Connectors

Board-to-board connectors are used to connect printed circuit boards (PCBs), an electronic component that contains a conductive pattern printed on the surface of the insulating base in an accurate and repeatable manner. Each terminal on a BTB connector is connected to a PCB. A BTB connector includes housing and a specific number of terminals.

Three different mounting types of board-to-board connectors are through hole, surface mount, and press fit technology. Two primary PCBs can be sandwiched or connected right angle with there connectors.

BTB connectors are selected by considering the mounting method, pin pitch, number of rows (a.k.a. number of ways), pin length, stacker height, etc.

Wire-to-Board Connectors

This type of device connects a wire to a printed circuit board (PCB), enabling connectivity between circuits. Manufactured for flexibility and reliability, wire-to-board connectors are engineered for low-profile mating and secure terminations, with products equipped with either a friction lock mechanism or a full lock mechanism. Multiple or single connection-type PCB tabs include stud mount, printed circuit mount, wire crimp, testing, weld, and adapters for quick disconnect applications.

Complex electromechanical system like drone may use many wire to board connectors across the system. For Example, the 360 degree view camera at the bottom of the drone may need a special cabling, which may not entangled when camera covers 360 degree. This should be flexible enough not to obstruct the camera view and allowing the camera to do a full rotation keeping the electrical contact stable.

RF Connectors

A coaxial RF connector (radio frequency connector) is an electrical connector designed to work at radio frequencies in the multi-megahertz range. RF connectors are typically used with coaxial cables and are designed to maintain the shielding that the coaxial design offers. Better models also minimize the change in transmission line impedance at the connection. Mechanically, they may provide a fastening mechanism (thread, bayonet, braces, blind mate) and springs for a low ohmic electric contact while sparing the gold surface, thus allowing very high mating cycles and reducing the insertion force. Research activity in the area of radio-frequency (RF) circuit design has surged in the 2000s in direct response to the enormous market demand for inexpensive, high-data-rate wireless transceivers.

FPC/FFC Connectors

FPC/FFC is a one-piece connector that makes the connection with a directly-inserted FFC or FPC and locks it by means of a lever. This type of connector can be used in a wide range of digital devices when a low profile or the horizontal insertion of flex is required.

Key Considerations

Generally speaking, electrical connectors are mechanical components that serve an electrical function. In addition to carrying electrical current at a specified voltage, connectors either enable interconnection of components during the assembly process or enable the user to easily disconnect and reconnect different parts of the equipment. The size and shape of connectors varies based upon the electrical requirements of the equipment, the physical space within the equipment, and environmental conditions in which the equipment must operate.

Connector manufacturers typically catalog connectors based upon interconnections, which refer to the connector application or mechanical method of interconnection. These applications range from connecting the chip to a circuit board to connecting peripherals to devices and beyond. Connectors that are attached to or mated with a printed circuit board comprise a large majority of catalog connector offerings.

Connectors are selected based on the following requirements:

- Application environment
- Electrical requirements
- Mechanical requirements
- Safety and regulatory requirements

Solutions

The selection of connectors is strictly based on the applications and the board form factor. There are multiple interconnects required for the board and the system.

Mechanicals

As discussed, several mechanical items must be added to complete the drone system. The key mechanical items are the quadcopter, propellers, enclosures, and mechanical interconnects. The quadcopter is the key component that decides the skeleton of the drone. Apart from these key mechanical components, there are numerous mechanicals inside the drone enclosures including the PCBA.

Categories

In any system design, the mechanical items are categorized into make or buy items. The quadcopter, plastic enclosures, and other customer parts inside the drone will be designed with the mechanical CAD tool in-house by the mechanical engineers. They are custom-made parts specific to the Crop monitoring drone.

Once the design is complete in the CAD tool, the files are shared with the manufacturers to prepare for the material and to manufacture the final component.

The other category is the buy items. Propellers, fans, landing gears, screws, and washers are usually buy items, and they can be purchased from the vendors directly by providing them requirements or specifications.

Key Considerations

The key considerations for selecting a quadcopter and the respective enclosure is as per the target dimensions, target weight, and other mechanical factors like board, camera module dimensions, and weight. For example, selecting a simple quadcopter has so many advantages over other multicopter designs:

- It's a simple design and the frame is easily available on the market for easy integration.

- They are less expensive than other multicopters.

- They are suitable for all kinds of flight functions like roll, pitch, yaw, and motion.

- The quadcopter can be done either with an X-frame or H-frame.

If there are readily less expensive quadcopters available in the market, this can be a buy item instead of make item. This reduces the effort and cost further for the drone makers.

Similarly, the enclosures and other mechanical components like landing gears, screws, and washers are selected based on the needs and included in the BOM for procurement as buy item. The only mechanical component that is very complicated and requires an expert's suggestion before purchase is the propellers.

Many commercially available motors and propellers are available for a drone. The key considerations are

- Lift: The drone should be able to provide two times the amount of thrust than the weight of the quadcopter. This includes the weight of the board and other mechanical components inside the drone.

- Size: The proper ratio of motor size to frame size.

- Power: The higher the voltage, the higher the speed of the motor. This means more power is necessary. There needs to be proper tradeoff between these features when selecting a propeller.

- Specs: Other specs of the motor like RPM, thrust, no load, and efficiency play a key role in the selection.

Solutions

Consider all the specs to pick the appropriate propellers for this drone. The camera can be fit on the bottom side of the drone to give a proper 360-degree view. An enclosure will cover all the parts of the drone except the propellers on the top and the camera on the bottom. The plastic enclosures will also cover the daughterboard on the top side and expose the antennas for better reachability.

Summary

In this chapter, you scanned through the ingredients selection and key considerations with a few examples of drone-specific ingredients. The process and procedure is same for any small component adding into the design at any stage. It is always the designer's responsibility to check the feasibility and select the best component from the different options. Apart from design considerations, the components must comply with industrial standards for industrial drones. And a general rule is that all components should be RoHS-compliant, which is restriction of hazardous substances on the component or in the manufacturing process of the component. This applicable for drone manufacturing also.

CHAPTER 4

Drone Hardware Development

In the previous chapter, you explored the key considerations for few of the essential ingredients of a drone. This chapter will explain how the electrical ingredients are put together to develop the hardware for the drone. At a high level, drone development can split into drone hardware development and drone system development. Drone hardware or PCBA development is a critical part of system development. The design or selection of components other than hardware completes the system design.

In any electronics system, the PCBA is considered as one single assembly item, particularly in a drone system, where the mechanical and electrical components play an equal and important role. Even then, hardware is the only item that goes through a complicated design process. Unlike the PCBA, other system-level ingredients are either easily procured or manufactured from dedicated suppliers.

PCBA development starts with the architecture, followed by the electrical ingredients selection, which was discussed in the previous chapters. The architecture and ingredients selections are the documentation part of the hardware development. The actual design requires electrical CAD tool involvement most of the time. The PCBA design process has several steps, which can go in parallel or sequential.

© Neeraj Kumar Singh, Porselvan Muthukrishnan, Satyanarayana Sanpini 2019
N. K. Singh et al., *Industrial System Engineering for Drones*,
https://doi.org/10.1007/978-1-4842-3534-8_4

The first step of the design is PCBA library development and the final step is getting a complete, functionally working PCBA. To get the final working PCBA, the total development cycle is split into design and validation cycles.

As mentioned earlier, this completed PCBA will be a single mechanical component assembled in a drone system.

PCB Library Development

PCB library development is the important task of PCB design and is a time-consuming task. It's usually done by highly trained professionals in all aspects of library management from creating library elements through to a complete library management environment. A library is usually managed in a central server or a cloud, which provides access to the components for several boards or projects at the same time.

Libraries are created in a specific file format and stored as individual files. Different tools use different file formats. Libraries created for a specific tool can't be interchanged with other tools. The electrical component library is a one-time creation process and will stay in the server forever. Each component created or newly added will have unique part identification in the same component library.

The entire library has to comply with the latest design technologies as well as standards such as IPC-7351B to ensure a high-quality library.

Symbol Creation

Library development is nothing but symbol creation for the required electrical components in the system. Two types of symbols are created by any board developers in hardware design. They are logical or schematics symbols and CAD symbols or PCB footprints.

A logical symbol is the visual representation of an electrical ingredient in the schematics. Similarly, a footprint is the visual representation of an electrical ingredient in a PCB layout.

Schematics are the visual representation of an electrical circuit. The completed schematic has all of the required symbols connected to each other with wires (nets) as per the design requirement.

The PCB layout is the visual representation of the actual PCB with all of the required PCB footprints connected to each other with copper traces in a multilayer PCB. The PCB layout is done with dimensions and scales matching the actual PCB and finally fabricated to a physical PCB.

Each individual component in the schematic has an individual logical symbol. One or more logical symbols can use same footprint, if the components share the same package. For example, the logical symbol for resistors is the same for all of the values. The designer has to pick the right value for their design. New resistor values are added to the same logical symbol and are maintained as component libraries whereas complex integrated circuits use unique logical symbols for each component. Technical specifications are added for each component along with other attributes like manufacturer part number and manufacturer name. The footprint is usually added as an attribute for the logical symbol.

Logical Symbol Creation

Every electrical CAD design software/project has a separate librarian tool to create, verify, and manage the component libraries. All symbols are created in a simple 2D plane with simple drawing tools like squares, rectangles, and circles. Discrete components such as resistors, capacitors, inductors, and diodes are created with their unique 2D representation with pins, which is commonly seen in text books. ICs are created as a square or rectangle box with pins attached to it.

A standard practice is to create the symbols with grids. Having grids in the symbols makes the schematic drawing easy; the schematic also should follow a similar grids. Symbols can be created in different styles. Generally, there are guidelines and BKMs (best known methods) to standardize the symbols and schematics for the whole organization.

Pin names and numbers typically match with the names and numbers from the component datasheet or the device collaterals. A few examples of logical symbols used in a drone power circuit are shown in Figure 4-1. Clockwise from the left corner is a resistor, capacitor, power, ground, inductor, and IC. All of the components shown in the architecture block diagram in Figure 2-2 have a corresponding logical symbol and footprint with all the associated discrete components.

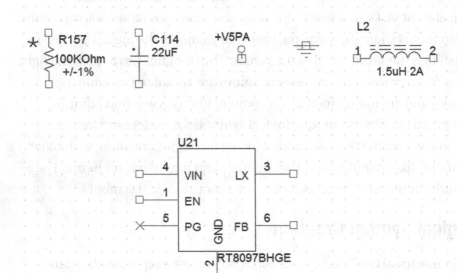

Figure 4-1. *Logical symbol examples*

Symbol Verification

Symbol verification is an important process associated with symbol creation. Once the symbol is created, it needs to be verified by the requested/concerned design engineer before adding it into the central library.

The created symbol should meet the standards and BKMs, and more importantly the symbol should be well-suited for the schematic design. The pins are arranged in such a way that the connections can be done with other peripheral components in a presentable manner and better readability.

So it is crucial to verify that the symbol is created as per the requirement. A symbol cannot be modified once it is added to the central library, which enables other board developers to use the same symbol for other boards and different projects.

PCB Footprint Creation

Similar to logical symbol creation, PCB footprint creation is done with a 2D electrical CAD tool with a simple drawing window. Unlike the logical symbol creation, footprint creation requires a different expertise. A footprint is the exact representation of component pads or a land pattern with proper scale. All footprints are also provided with component height information to generate a 3D view from a layout file if needed.

The footprint is the exact replica of the component pads including dimensions, unlike the logical symbol, which is the only visual representation of the component in a schematic.

A footprint is the visual representation of the component in a PCB layout. The fabricated bare PCB will have all the component pads, exactly created as a footprint on which the components are mounted. This bare PCB with all the components mounted completes the hardware and provides a finished PCBA.

Figure 4-2 shows a completed layout with all the component footprints. Footprints are red for resistors, purple for capacitors, yellow for inductors, and green for IC. Every block in the drone architecture block diagram in Figure 2-2 has a PCB footprint with an associated discrete component.

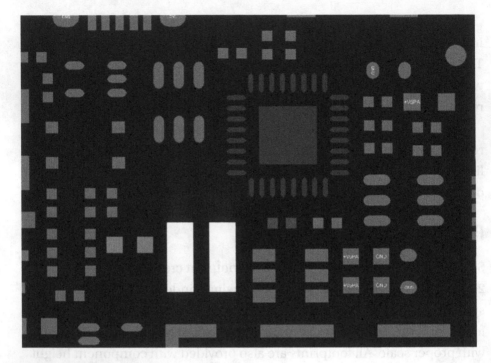

Figure 4-2. *PCB footprint examples*

Footprint Verification

Footprint verification is also a critical process, similar to the logical symbol verification. Generally, there are multiple levels of verification done to check the footprint compliance with the IPC guidelines. The footprint is added in the library and accessed by board developers through the component libraries.

Schematics Design

Schematics design is the representation of the detailed electrical circuit elements interconnection within a system. Schematics give a detailed view of the components and the connections between them. It's the precise low-level design of the hardware block diagram shown in the Figure 4-3.

116

Every electrical component of the system is placed on the schematic and connected with other components logically and functionally as per the design. Schematics are done considering all the electrical rules, laws, and guidelines for proper operation. Generally, schematic designs are produced by professional analog and deigital electronics design engineers.

Schematics Capture

The drone architecture diagram in Figure 2-2 is converted to a multiple page electrical circuit in a schematics capture. A simple hardware circuit with fewer components can be accommodated on a single page. A complex hardware circuit like a drone can't be done on a single page. Multiple pages show multiple components connected across the pages. Connections across the pages are always presented with off-page connectors.

All the connections are labelled with net names for easy identification on the layout. Connections without net names are provided with random names and numbers when generating net list. This helps engineers identify and understand the electrical connection and types on a layout tool after importing the schematics files in a layout.

Connections are usually divided into power, ground, and signals. Signals are classified as analog, digital, and RF signals. Digital signals are further classified as high speed and low speed signals. Each connection or interface follows the set of electrical guidelines for connections and terminations. These signal terminations are represented in schematics with appropriate components like resistors, inductors, and capacitors on the actual connection.

In a schematic, each component is provided with a unique reference designator. This reference designator helps to identify the particular component throughout the hardware development especially in layout, bill of materials, testing, and validation.

In addition to the component datasheet, every component manufacturer provides a recommended design. This recommended design is based on the evaluation board design and tested data from the manufacturer. However, a designer can choose to design a completely new circuit that is different from the reference circuit. An example schematic of a power component is shown in Figure 4-3.

There are numerous complicated circuit designs for the complete drone hardware, interconnected to each other on multi-page schematics, which may or may not follow the reference circuit from the datasheet.

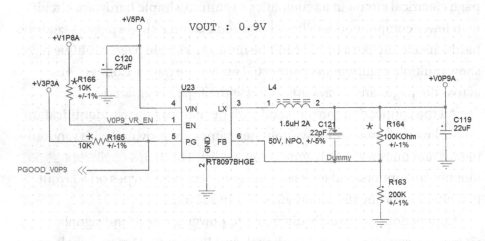

Figure 4-3. *Schematics example*

Design Rules Checking

Design Rules Checking (DRC) is a powerful automated feature that checks both the logical and physical integrity of a design. Checks are made against any or all enabled *design rules* embedded in the tool. The tool generates reports and suggestions.

This feature should be used on every schematic to show that electrical rules have been maintained and to ensure there are no other design violations. It is particularly recommended that a design rule check always be performed prior to generating the final netlist.

118

There are also tools available for circuit simulation. Simulation allows the designer to check the circuit operation. However, simulation requires the actual electrical model of the components or the schematic needs to be exported to other simulation tools with all of the electrical specifications of the component.

Generating a Netlist

Netlist generation is the final step in the schematic design. In electronic design, a netlist is a description of the connectivity of an electronic circuit. In its simplest form, a netlist consists of a list of the electronic components in a circuit and a list of the nodes they are connected to. A network (net) is a collection of two or more interconnected components.

The structure, complexity, and representation of a netlist can vary considerably, but the fundamental purpose of every netlist is to convey connectivity information. Netlists usually provide nothing more than instances, nodes, and perhaps some attributes of the components involved.

For the Crop monitoring drone, three different schematics and netlists are generated. One is for the main board, one for the daughterboard, and one for the flex PCB board.

Bill of Materials

The bill of materials (BOM) is a key data set generated from a board design project either from a schematic or a layout tool. This report-type document provides a listing of all components required to build the product, including the bare board, which is essentially the base "component" upon which all other parts are assembled. The BOM acts as a guide for what needs to be procured to build the product as designed. It also provides a means to calculate the cost based on the required number of assembled boards in a requested spin. The BOM is generated through a dedicated and powerful report generation engine, the interface of which is known as the Report Manager from the tool itself.

An electrical BOM can be in a spreadsheet format with attributes in each column. Attributes are usually provided for each component while creating the logical symbol.

The schematics entry tool provides the options to generate the BOM in multiple formats.

Since creating a schematic is a manual, time-consuming process, a BOM is generated frequently from the partially completed schematics. This partial BOM is called an intermediate demand BOM, and it's sent to the PCBA manufacturing factory. The factory communicates to the suppliers and requests the components and required quantities.

Early submission of the demand BOM is better for long lead components. This enables the supplier to get the required quantities from their side to meet the PCBA manufacturing schedule. Figure 4-4 shows an example of a tool-generated BOM.

For the drone design, three different electrical BOMs are generated for the motherboard, daughterboard, and flex PCB.

			BILL OF MATERIAL						
REV OF BOM			Customer P/N		Marketing Name			DATE	
SMT P/N					Product Code			Remark	
Item	Description	Supplier	Supplier P/N	Usage	Item Status	Location	Value	Footprint	Package Type
1	CAP,3.3nF,+/-10%,X7R,50V,G,SMD0402	YAGEO	CC0402KRX7R9BB332	1	E	BC1	3.3nF	c0402h6	SMD
	CAP,3.3nF,+/-10%,X7R,50V,G,SMD0402	MURATA	GRM155R71H332K		E				SMD
	CAP,3.3nF,+/-10%,X7R,50V,G,SMD0402	DARFON	C10005X7R332KGT		E				SMD
	CAP,3.3nF,+/-10%,X7R,50V,G,SMD0402	WALSIN	0402B332K500CT		E				SMD
2	LED,Blue,APT1608LVBC/D,5V,2mA,G,SMD0603	KINGBRIGHT	APT1608LVBC/D	1	E	D1	LED_BLUE	leds2p16x8h8	SMD
	LED,Blue,B1911NB--02D-003414,5V,2mA,G,SMD0603	HARVATEK	B1911NB--02D-003414		E				SMD
3	DIODE,TVS,PESD12VL1BA,G,SOD323-2,SMD	NXP	PESD12VL1BA	2	E	D6,D7	PESD12VL1BA	sod323_1h11	SMD
	DIODE,TVS,PESD12VL1BA,G,SOD323-2,SMD	NEXPERIA	PESD12VL1BA		E				SMD
4	TVS Diode,AZ2025-01H,R7G,SOD-523,2P,G	AMAZING	AZ2025-01H,R7G	2	E	D9,D14	AZ2025-01H,R7G	sod_523_np	SMD
5	FB,120 Ohm@100MHz,+/-25%,3A,25mOhm,G,SMD0603	MURATA	BLM185G121TN1D	1	E	FB8	FB120 Ohm	0603h7	SMD
	FB,120 Ohm@100MHz,+/-25%,3A,30mOhm,G,SMD0603	CHILISIN	UPB160808T-121Y-N		E				SMD
	FB,120 Ohm@100MHz,+/-25%,3A,40mOhm,G,SMD0603	TAI-TECH	HCB1608VF-121T30		E				SMD
	IND,2.4nH@100MHz,+/-0.3nH,400mA,150mOhm,G,SMD0402	CHILISIN	CLH1005T-2N4S-S		E				SMD
	IND,2.4nH@100MHz,+/-0.3nH,300mA,150mOhm,G,SMD0402	MURATA	LQG15HS2N4S02D		E				SMD
6	RES,27 Ohm,+/-5%,1/16W,G,SMD0402	WALSIN	WR04X270JTL	4	E	R206,R207,R208,R209	27	r0402h4	SMD
	RES,27 Ohm,+/-5%,1/16W,G,SMD0402	YAGEO	RC0402JR-0727RL		E				SMD
	RES,27 Ohm,+/-5%,1/16W,G,SMD0402	TA-I	RM04JTh270		E				SMD
7	IC,Regulator,RT8097BHGE,ADJ,2A,G,SOT-23-6,SMD	RICHTEK	RT8097BHGE	2	E	U21,U22	RT8097BHGE	sot23_6_1h15	SMD
8	IC,Switch,SN74LVC1G66DRLR,1.65V~5.5V,G,SOT-1123-5,SMD	TI	SN74LVC1G66DRLR	1	E	U24	SN74LVC1G66DRL	sot553_5h6	SMD
9	CONN,I/O,Audio jack,R/A,Bla,3.15mm,3u,G,SMD-6	SINGATRON	2SJ2269-002111	1	E	U26	2SJ2269-002111	phone_jack5h44	SMD
10	Logic IC,Translator,SN74AUP1T34DCKR,0.9V~3.6V,45.65ns,SC-70/SO	TI	SN74AUP1T34DCKR	1	E	U27	SN74AUP1T34DCK	sc70_5h11	SMD
11	XTAL,40MHz,+/-10ppm,15pF,G,SMD	TXC	8Z40000022	1	E	XTAL1	XTAL_40MHz	x4s26x21h6	SMD
12	XTAL,38.4MHz,+/-10ppm,12pF,G,SMD	TXC	8Q38470013	1	E	X1	XATL-38.4MHz	x4s16x12h4	SMD

Figure 4-4. *Tool-generated BOM*

Symbol Attributes

There are certain inputs to be taken care in a schematics tool to generate a BOM. The key inputs are symbol attributes. General BKM is to provide all the symbol attributes while creating a logical symbol itself. Figure 4-5 shows the symbol attribute window from a schematics tool. The first column shows the attribute names, and the corresponding symbol attributes are provided in the second column. A complete, clean BOM can be generated from the schematic if the logical symbol is provided with all the required properties in a BOM.

	A
Color	Default
Description	Linear IC,Regulator,RT
Designator	
Foxconn Part Number	32014J900-264-G
Graphic	RT8097BLGE_0.Normal
ID	
Implementation	
Implementation Path	
Implementation Type	<none>
Location X-Coordinate	760
Location Y-Coordinate	465
Mfg	RICHTEK
Mfg Part Number	RT8097BHGE
Name	INS17967383
Package Type	SMD
Part Reference	U23
PCB Footprint	sot23_6_1h15
Power Pins Visible	⌐
Primitive	DEFAULT
Reference	U23
Remark	Reserved
Source Package	RT8097BLGE_0
Source Part	RT8097BLGE_0.Norm
Value	RT8097BHGE
VPN	32014J900-VPN-G

Figure 4-5. *Symbol attribute window*

BOM Generation

A BOM can be generated from the project source documents or from the active PCB document using the Reports > Bill of Materials command from the schematic or PCB editor.

The tool-generated BOM is shared with the PCBA manufacturer to add additional information required for the BOM, usually local supplier and cost data. Being able to cost a project and determine the quantities of design components to be ordered from suppliers/distributors is an essential part of the overall design process.

The following supplier-based data can be included in a bill of materials by the factory. Designers can also add this data into the tool-generated BOM itself, if they have access to all this information from suppliers or factory.

- *Supplier*: Name of the supplier

- *Supplier currency*: Alphabetic code for the chosen currency used for pricing data. Usually US dollars for most suppliers.

- *Supplier order quantity*: Number of units required to fulfill the desired production quantity of the product.

- *Supplier part number*: Part number for the supplier item. This is different from the manufacturing part number.

- *Supplier stock*: How many units of the item the supplier has in stock.

- *Supplier subtotal*: The supplier order quantity multiplied by the supplier unit price, resulting in the subtotal for that item.

- *Supplier unit price*: Cost per unit of the supplier item.

Material Readiness

Keeping the materials ready for the PCBA is a complicated process in any factory. Each component needs to be checked frequently and followed up with the supplier for stock. Once the design is fixed for one particular part number, it cannot be modified after fabricating the board.

There may be some footprint-compatible components available from the same vendor or competitive vendor. But getting the stock at the right time is difficult and so is meeting the schedule.

Layout Design

The completed schematic circuit of the design is transformed into a PCB. The netlist from the schematic is imported into the layout tool as the base. The electrical components need to be grouped and placed in order to comply with all the electrical guidelines when routing the signals.

The PCB layout can be performed manually (using CAD) or in combination with an auto route. The best results are usually still achieved using at least some manual routing, simply because the design engineer has a far better judgement of how to arrange circuitry. Many auto-routed boards are often completely illogical in their track routing; the program has optimized the connections and sacrificed any small amount of order that may have been put in place by manual routing.

The CAD PCB layout consists of several layers; for illustration, often the layers are colored and compressed into the one overlay image. The circuit design and the PCB overlay image are usually supplied by the designer to the client in a PDF document produced by the CAD package. The PCB overlay may quite easily be printed in the actual size, cut out, and used for approximate size comparisons with mechanical items. For instance, the print can be placed inside the actual enclosure to see how it will be positioned in relation to other parts. Components can also be placed up against the pad markings as a quick idiot-check of dimensions.

The width of the tracks is a trade-off based on current flow, space available, size of parts, and electromagnetic interference. The track layout is a similar trade-off that also picks when to dodge from one side of the board to the other to avoid an obstacle, but overall normally aims to find the shortest regular path between the connected points. Given the impedance, susceptibility, and signal on tracks, the loop area is another trade-off that is considered as the design proceeds. Added to all this is the design for manufacture.

Board Outline

For a drone, one possible shape is a rectangular board, considering the mechanical structure. But it's not uncommon to see round, triangular, or other interesting PCB shapes. Drone PCBs are designed to be as small as possible, but that's not necessary if your application doesn't require it.

If you are putting the PCB into a drone enclosure, the dimensions may be limited by the size of the housing. In that case, you need to know the enclosure's dimensions before laying out the PCB so that everything fits inside. As seen in the second chapter, the ID defines the size of the PCB and outline.

The various components also have an effect on the size of the finished PCB. For instance, surface-mounted components are small and have a low profile, so you'll be able to make the PCB smaller. Through hole components are larger, but they're often easier to find and solder.

Layer Stack-Up

Larger circuits can be difficult to design on a single- or double-layer PCB. Most of the component packages are BGA packages, which need signals to be routed in an internal layer. Considering the density of the signals and complexity of the routing, you might need multiple layers with different layer vias to achieve the smallest size. A first-level initial assessment is done during the architecture phase, as seen in Chapter 2, and is carried forward to the actual layout design, with modifications if required.

Most PCB manufacturers let you order different layer thicknesses. "Copper weight" is the term manufacturers use to describe the layer thickness, and it's measured in ounces. The thickness of a layer will affect how much current can flow through the circuit without damaging the traces. Trace width is another factor that affects how much current can safely flow through the circuit. To determine safe values for width and thickness, you need to know the amperage that will flow through the trace in question. An online trace width calculator can help determine the ideal trace thickness and width for a given amperage.

Generally, multiple layer PCBs have few continuous ground layers where the entire layer is covered with a copper plane connected to ground. The positive traces are routed on top and connections to ground are made with through holes or vias. Ground layers are good for circuits that are prone to interference because the large area of copper acts as a shield against electromagnetic fields. They also help dissipate the heat generated by the components.

Electrical Constraints

In a professionally designed PCB, most of the copper traces bend at 45° angles. One reason for this is that 45° angles shorten the electrical path between components compared to 90° angles. Another reason is that high-speed logic signals can get reflected off the back of the angle, causing interference.

This drone project uses digital logic or high-speed communication protocols above 200 MHz. All general high-speed guidelines are applicable, like avoiding 90° angles and vias in the traces. For slower speed circuits, 90° traces won't have much of an effect on the performance of your circuit.

Like layer thickness, the width of your traces will affect how much current can flow through your circuit without damaging the circuit.

The proximity of traces to components and adjacent traces will also determine how wide your traces can be. When designing a small PCB with lots of traces and components, you might need to make the traces narrow for everything to fit.

Signal Integrity

The challenges of high-speed design require some additional effort to ensure signal integrity. This can be achieved by following fundamental analog design rules and using careful PCB layout techniques.

A transmission line can be defined as a "conductive connection between a transmitter and a receiver capable of carrying a signal." Traditionally, transmission lines are thought of as telecom-based cables operating over long distances. However, with high-speed digital signal transmission, even the shortest passive PCB track suffers from transmission line effects. At low frequencies, a wire or a PCB track may be considered to be an ideal circuit without resistance, capacitance, or inductance. But at high frequencies, AC circuit characteristics dominate, causing impedances, inductances, and capacitances to become prevalent in the wire.

Impedance Mismatch

Unequal impedance of the source output, line, receiver, or load causes impedance mismatch. This mismatch means the transmitted signal is not fully absorbed within the receiver and the excess energy is reflected back to the transmitter. This process continues back and forth until all of the energy is absorbed. At high data rates, this can cause signal overshoot, undershoot, ringing, and stair-step waveforms, which produce signal errors. Impedance mismatch can be overcome by matching the transceiver buffers to the transmission media. In the case of a PCB, this can be achieved by careful selection of the medium and by the use of termination schemes.

The termination scheme used to overcome impedance mismatch depends on the application. The schemes include simple parallel termination and more complex RC termination where a resistor capacitor network provides a low pass filter to remove low frequency effects but passes the high frequency signal.

Signal Attenuation

High-frequency signal transmission line losses make it difficult for the receiver to interpret the information correctly. The following two types of transmission line losses are due to the transmission medium:

- *Dielectric absorption*: High-frequency signals excite molecules in the insulator, which cause the insulator to absorb signal energy. This absorption reduces the signal strength. Dielectric absorption relates to the PCB material and can be lessened by careful material selection.

- *Skin effect*: Varying current waveforms caused by AC and high-frequency signals tend to travel on the conductor's surface. Signals traveling on the surface cause the self-inductance of the material to produce an increased inductive reactance at high frequencies, which forces electrons to the material's surface. The effective reduction of the conductive area causes an increase of resistance and, therefore, attenuation of the signal. Increasing track width can reduce the skin effect, but this is not always possible.

Cross Talk

Whenever a signal is driven along a wire, a magnetic field develops around the wire. If two wires are placed adjacent to each other, it is possible that the two magnetic fields interact, causing a cross-coupling of energy between signals known as crosstalk. The following two energy coupling types are the predominant causes of crosstalk:

- *Mutual inductance*: A magnetic field causes induced current from the driven wire to appear on the quiet wire. This mutual inductance causes positive waves to appear near the transmitter end of the quiet line (near end inductance) and negative waves at the receiver end of the transmission line (far end crosstalk).

- *Mutual capacitance*: The coupling of two electric fields when current is injected in the quiet line proportional to the rate of change of voltage in the driver. This mutual capacitance causes positive waves near both ends of the transmission line.

Power Integrity

Power integrity (PI) is an analysis to check whether the desired voltage and current requirements are met from source to destination. Today, power integrity plays a major role in the success and failure of new electronic products. There are several coupled aspects of PI: on the chip, on the chip package, on the circuit board, and in the system. Four main issues must be resolved to ensure power integrity at the printed circuit board level:

- Keep the voltage ripple at the chips pads lower than the specification.

- Control ground bounce (also called synchronous switching noise, simultaneous switching noise, or simultaneous switching output).

- Control electromagnetic interference and maintain electromagnetic compatibility: the power distribution network is generally the largest set of conductors on the circuit board and therefore the largest antenna for emission and reception of noise.

- Maintaining a proper DC voltage level at the load at high currents is challenging. A modern processor or field-programmable gate array can draw 1-100 Amps at sub-1V VDD levels with AC and DC margins in the tens of millivolts. Very little DC voltage drop can thus be tolerated on the power distribution network.

The current path from the power supply through the PCB and IC package to the die is called the power distribution network. Its role is to transfer the power to the consumers with little DC voltage drop and to allow little ripple induced by dynamic current at the consumer. The DC drop occurs if there is too much resistance in the plane or power traces leading from the VR to the load. This can be countered by raising the voltage on the VR or extending the "sense" point of the VR to the consumer.

Dynamic current occurs when the consumer switches its transistors, typically triggered by a clock. This dynamic current can be considerably larger than the static current (internal leakage) of the consumer. This fast current consumption can pull the voltage of the rail down, creating a voltage ripple. This change in current happens much faster than the VRM can react. The switching current must therefore be handled by decoupling capacitors.

The noise or voltage ripple must be handled differently depending on the frequency of operation. The highest frequencies must be handled on-die. This noise is decoupled by parasitic coupling on the die and capacitive coupling between metal layers. Frequencies above 50-100 MHz must be handled on the package; this is done by on-package capacitors. Frequencies below 100 MHz are handled on the PCB by plane capacitance and using decoupling capacitors. Capacitors work on different frequencies depending on their type, capacitance, and physical size. It is therefore necessary to utilize multiple capacitors of different sizes to ensure low PDN impedance across the frequency range. The physical size of the capacitors affects its parasitic inductance. The parasitic inductance creates impedance spikes at certain frequencies. Smaller capacitors are therefore better. The placement of the capacitors is of varying importance depending on the frequency of operation. The smallest value capacitors should be as close as possible to the consumer to minimize the AC current loop area. Larger capacitors in the micro Farad range can be placed more or less anywhere.

The target impedance is the impedance at which the ripple created by the dynamic current of the specific consumer is within the specified range. In addition to the target impedance, it is important to know which frequencies it applies, and at which frequency the consumer package is responsible (this is specified in the datasheet of the specific consumer IC).

Mechanical Constraints

One of the more challenging parts of managing today's electronic product development process is collaboration among various players of a project. PCB designers often find themselves negotiating between industrial or mechanical designers and electrical designers. Requirements from each team may conflict, and often the PCB designer must resolve these differences.

The most important step for a mechanical designer and a PCB designer is to agree on the ground rules for working together. Establishing a common coordinate system, orientation, dimensioning, and units are key to getting off to a good start.

Compared to mechanical CAD programs, PCB design software has very limited mechanical design capabilities:

- Most PCB design software can only view a board in a single orientation and from a single direction. Boards are viewed from a single side, and opposite side features and components are viewed as an "X-ray" through the board.

- PCB design software typically has much less flexible dimensioning capabilities. In particular, most PCB software lacks the automatic linked-in dimensioning that mechanical CAD users take for granted.

- Most PCB design software has less flexibility in measuring and documenting distances between features. Even the lowest-cost mechanical CAD software implements extensive relative measurements and features "snap to" capabilities.

Coordinate System

In the circuit board industry, it is standard to place the origin at the lower left-hand corner of the circuit board, with the horizontal axis as the X axis and the vertical axis as the Y axis. Some designers prefer to use the lower left mounting or tooling hole as the origin. For boards with cutouts or chamfers in that corner, place the origin where the corner would have been without the cutout or at either remaining corner. For circular or radially-symmetrical boards, place the origin at the center of the board. Establishing a useful origin for unusual shaped boards may call for some creativity.

Orientation

If practical, orient the longest axis horizontally to allow the largest view area on a standard landscape computer monitor. Create all board drawings from the same viewpoint, unless there are compelling reasons to show them in another orientation. If drawings need to be viewed from the reverse "mirrored" side, be sure to keep the same origin and provide notes to help the designer definitively establish which edge is which.

Dimension

PCB designers are used to working with coordinate dimensions. Writing all dimensions in ordinate style removes a common source of error by eliminating the need to do math to figure out feature and component locations.

Keep Out Zones (KOZ)

The mechanical designer needs to communicate the following to the PCB designer:

- *Board physical description*: Shape of the board, including slots, cutouts, and thickness, location and diameter of mounting and tooling holes.

- *Design constraints*: Maximum component height for both sides and keep-out areas.

- *Location and part numbers of critical components, especially connectors*: Except for the simplest of boards, this is a lot of information to place in a single drawing. Cluttered drawings can be difficult to make and error-prone to read. When in doubt, create separate drawings for different information. Be sure to keep the orientation consistent and unambiguous!

Physical Constraints

Draw the shape of the board to scale and detail slots, cut-outs, chamfers, mounting/tooling holes, and hole clearances. For curved sections, show the center point and radius, plus the location of the curve end-points. PCBs are milled to shape so concave corners need to be rounded. If there are board dimensions that can be expanded or shrunk, indicate them on the drawing. Be sure to note the required board thickness (0.062", 0.093", and 0.031" thicknesses are few common thicknesses). Creating a system-level drawing can be a great way to communicate physical constraints. Show the board superimposed on an enclosure or in relation to other boards in a system.

Design Constraints

Indicate design constraints such as whether parts may be placed on both sides and the maximum component heights for each side. Show areas that need to be free of components or free of traces. Place an arrow and a note on the drawing to indicate the direction of system airflow.

Component Location

Specifying component locations can be one of the more challenging parts of a PCB design project. The geometric center is the best reference point for many parts such as chip resistors, capacitors, diodes, transistors, and ICs. However, other components such as connectors don't always have obvious points of reference. Here are some guidelines:

- Use the geometric center of the mating surface as the reference point for vertical mount connectors.

- For right-angle connectors, dimension the center line and front edge.

- For through-hole connectors, include a set of reference dimensions for at least one pin (pin 1). Note that using the pad as a reference point does not always work for surface mount parts as the pad center may not correspond to either the pin or lead center.

- For all connectors, show the relative position of both pin 1 and pin 2.

- For FFC/FPC (flat flex cable/flat printed circuit) connectors, indicate the cable conductive side and cable plug-in direction. In general, don't be anxious about including additional "reference" dimensions. When in doubt, add a note explaining the chosen reference points.

It is important to set up the board outline, stack-up, electrical, and mechanical constraints before importing the netlist. All of these constraints are general and a few might be more relevant to the drone design.

Netlist

The netlist is the final output file from the schematic and is also a primary input for a PCB layout.

The instances, nodes, and attributes of the components involved and the connections are imported into the layout tool. Once the components are imported, they can be either placed manually or automatically.

Placement

Components are grouped together based on the functionality and placed closer to each other to reduce the length of the signal routing.

Figure 4-6 shows an IC highlighted in blue placed inside the board outline. Associated components highlighted in green for that IC are grouped together outside the board before being placed inside the board outline. Other components (in grey) imported from the netlist are already grouped and placed inside the board outline.

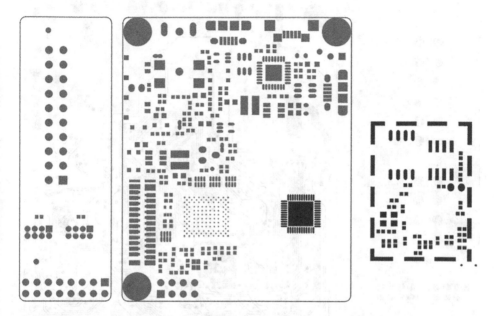

Figure 4-6. *A PCB CAD file with partially completed placement*

Routing

Once the placement is done, placement review is done by the electrical designers to check the placement as per the electrical guidelines. CAD engineers start routing the signals after placement completion. Routing is done layer by layer, interface by interface. Electrical properties of the signals are provided in the constraint manager based on the type of the signal. Different routing is required for different signal types. The trace width and max length of the signal vary based on the layers used.

Figure 4-7 shows the partially routed internal layer in a placement completed board. The net highlighted in blue on the south side is not routed. It needs to be routed with spacing as per the guidelines with other nets. The signal net has to meet trace impedance requirement.

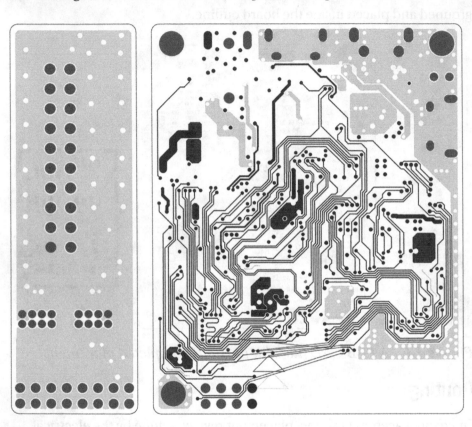

Figure 4-7. *A PCB with partially completed routing*

Mechanical Check

A CAD engineer can generate certain files from the electrical CAD tools for mechanical engineers. These files are required for a mechanical engineer to generate a 3D view of the PCB assembly.

This 3D view of the PCB assembly is in certain standard file format, which can be imported to any mechanical tool to check the mechanical assembly of the drone with other mechanical components already imported to the tool or designed in the same tool.

Gerber Release

Initially developed by a company with the name of Gerber, the Gerber format currently refers to a widely accepted standard capable of describing board images such as conductor layers, solder mask layers, and legend layers.

Printed circuit boards are designed in a specialized EDA (electronic design automation) or a CAD system that further generates board manufacturing data, based on which circuit board fabrications are commenced. PCB manufacturers won't fully understand all details of a PCB design file unless a Gerber format file is generated for reference and guidelines. The Gerber format file is applied to describe the design requirement of each image of a circuit board and it can be applied for both bare board fabrication and PCB assembly.

No one needs a delayed printed circuit board project. Delayed PCBs often end in huge penalties paid to the manufacture for the wasted slots. The ideal circumstance is that you send your design file to the PCB manufacturer, and the manufacturer arranges board fabrication based on your file and delivers the products to you. The practical situation, however, is not that simple.

It usually takes a long period of time from the moment you send your design file out to the final arrival of the boards. Certain effectiveness and efficiency measures can spare you from unwanted delays in PCB manufacturing.

When it comes to bare board fabrication, the Gerber format is called for by both standard photo plotters and other manufacturing equipment desiring image data like legend printers, direct imagers, or

AOI (automated/automatic optical inspection) equipment. Put simply, Gerber format files are essential from the beginning to the end of the PCB fabrication process.

When it comes to PCB assembly, a stencil layer is included in the Gerber format and component locations are regulated as well, which are regarded as significant reference data for SMT (surface mount technology) assembly, thru-hole assembly, and mix of them.

Gerber files do play a crucial role as a connector and translator between PCB design engineers and PCB manufacturers, enabling design engineers' considerations and concepts to be understood by manufacturers so that correct and reliable products can be effectively and efficiently manufactured.

Summary

In this chapter, we discussed general and drone-specific hardware development procedures and processes. The hardware development cycle starts with the architecture block diagram, but the actual detailed design starts from the library creation and schematic design for the multiple boards in the system. Completed schematics are transferred to the layout tool with appropriate inputs and prerequisites. The prerequisites for the layout define the outline, stack-up, and the electrical and mechanical constraints. Finally, the Gerber release for all the boards required for the drone marks the end of the drone hardware design cycle, which is the half mile crossed for the entire development cycle.

CHAPTER 5

System Assembly, Bring-Up and Validation

The second half of the product development cycle is the board bring-up, which aids the final system bring-up. No physical hardware or system parts are seen until the Gerber release. That is when the bring-up, the actual hardware, and mechanical parts are available for hands-on. The upcoming chapters will discuss more about the manufacturing, power on, testing, and validation of the actual hardware and the system. The pilot system build starts once the system is tested and validated against all the design and certification requirements as per the PRD. The system is deployed with the features list. Pilot systems are usually distributed to internal customers and are restricted to a lab environment until the system passes the regulatory and precompliance testing. Feedback and input from customers are consolidated to fine-tune the system further. Often, there is a separate tool for bug assignment, tracking, and issue resolution.

Regulatory and environmental compliance testing is required for any electronic product. The presence of wireless radios and other communication modules on the system makes it mandatory to pass more stringent compliance standards. Apart from the usual commercial

© Neeraj Kumar Singh, Porselvan Muthukrishnan, Satyanarayana Sanpini 2019
N. K. Singh et al., *Industrial System Engineering for Drones*,
https://doi.org/10.1007/978-1-4842-3534-8_5

and industrial electronic product certifications, flying an unmanned aerial vehicle (drone) means compliance with additional standards and regulations specified by the Federal Aviation Authority (FAA).

This chapter covers the manufacturing and assembly of the drone with the list of make and buy items ordered as per the system BOM. PCBs are the primary make item; they are designed in-house and manufactured by the PCB vendors using a complex manufacturing and assembly process.

PCB Fabrication Process

For most of the electronics system design, the PCB manufacturing, assembly, and bring-up process is the same. The PCB manufacturing process starts immediately after releasing the Gerber files to the PCB fabricator. Design engineers will clear any engineering questions raised by the manufacturer after the initial assessment of the Gerber files. The fabrication process starts after clearing all the engineering questions. The design and layout engineers are not involved in the PCB fabrication, but it is always good to have working knowledge of the process and design for manufacturing (DFM) concepts. Knowledge of these concepts will improve the quality of the deliverables in forthcoming PCB designs; this will also avoid repetitive mistakes and reduce the number of engineering questions.

Fabrication Steps

PCB manufacturing companies have specific manufacturing processes depending on the technologies used by the PCB vendor. In a multilayer PCB, layers of copper foil, prepreg, and core material are sandwiched together, as shown in the layer stack-up in Chapter 2. The multiple layers are pressed together under high temperature and pressure. High pressure and temperature will melt the prepreg adhesive that holds the multiple layers into a single PCB.

The standard manufacturing steps for a simple double-layer PCB are as follows:

1. Cut the PCB raw materials to a suitable size and shape.

2. Drill the PCB for mounting holes and vias as per the drill file (part of the design package).

3. Plate the drilled holes with copper (thickness as specified by the design engineers).

4. Press the board with dry film.

5. Transfer the routing to the board by exposing the dry film and route film on the top. (The routing is unique for each layer.)

6. Put the board in the electric copper machine to make the board conductive.

7. Add electric tin to take away the copper protected by the dry film.

8. Take away the dry film.

9. Use a special liquid to etch the unused copper on the board.

10. Remove the tin.

11. Apply a solder mask on the board, which is an epoxy resin and is normally green in color (this is the material that gives the green color to the PCB).

12. Expose the solder mask on the component pads for soldering (top and bottom layer).

13. Print the silk screen.

141

14. Finish the surface.

15. Perform the flying probe test.

16. Run functional and quality checks.

17. Package and ship the bare PCB to the assembly house.

For a multilayer PCB, the layers are finished individually and pressed together in the proper sequence with the correct orientation as per the design file. The multilayer sandwiched board is then electroplated on the top and bottom layers with the required copper thickness. The board continues from Step 2 of the PCB process for the top and bottom layers.

The manufacturer can also do a multipack fabrication as per the designer's request, if the PCB size is small. A multipack PCBA combines two or more identical PCBAs, fabricated and assembled in a single PCB substrate. A multipack can also be done for different PCBAs with the same layer stack-up. A multipack configuration increases the output and reduces the cost.

Different types of materials are used for core and prepreg on the internal layers of a multilayer PCB. The top and bottom layers are usually thick copper foils electroplated with copper too. The total copper thickness of the top and bottom layer is the combined thickness of the copper foil and plating.

The finished thickness of the board is usually +/- 10% from most of the PCB fabricators. The final board is packed and shipped for the SMT (surface mount technology) assembly process.

PCB Assembly Process

Unlike the fabrication, the assembly process needs significant involvement from the design engineers. As described in previous chapters, the production BOM (electrical BOM) is the final input for the PCB assembly. The multilayer bare PCB shipped from the fabricator is one of the line items of the production BOM.

The system BOM can include multiple PCBAs (for example, motherboard, daughterboard, flex PCBs, etc. in a Crop Squad drone kind of system). Each PCBA of the system has to go through the same fabrication and assembly process individually.

PCBA manufacturers also assess the functionality of a PCB design; this primarily includes a DFM check. This is a preliminary step; the training and knowledge transfer occurs between the design engineers and manufacturers before the real PCBA process even begins.

Most companies specializing in PCB assembly need the design file of the PCB to start out, along with any other design notes and specific requirements. For more complicated designs, the designers release the pre-Gerber files as a trial package, before releasing the actual Gerber files, so that the PCB assembly company can check the PCB file for any issues that may affect the PCB's functionality or manufacturability. This activity captures design for manufacturability issues, short circuits, or any other electrical problems.

This check also covers the design specifications of a PCB. More specifically, it looks for any missing, redundant, or potentially problematic features. Any of these issues may severely and negatively influence the functionality of the final project. For example, one common PCB design flaw is leaving too little spacing between PCB components, which can result in shorts and other malfunctions.

By identifying potential problems through DFM checks before manufacturing begins, you can cut manufacturing costs and eliminate unanticipated expenses. This is because these checks cut down on the low-yield issues.

Boards can be powered on immediately after the assembly. There are some key steps to be followed to get the board ready for power-on. They are manual, best known methods, followed traditionally in any PCBA bring-up process.

Surface Mount Assembly Process

The surface mount assembly process is the assembly of the surface mount devices on a PCB. There are a wide range of SMD component packages available on the market and they come in various shapes and sizes; for example, BGA, QFN, and LGA are different varieties of SMT packages offered for an IC.

Surface mount technology was developed to build highly complex electronic circuits into smaller and smaller assemblies with good repeatability and with a higher level of automation. SMT reduces the manufacturing costs and enables the engineers to use the PCB space more efficiently. There are step-by-step processes necessary to complete an SMT of a PCB.

Solder Paste Stenciling

Applying a solder paste to the board is the first step of the assembly process. A thin stainless-steel stencil is placed over the PCB, which is similar to placing a mask in a screen printing process. This allows technicians to apply solder paste only to certain pads of the target PCB. These pads are where components will sit on the finished PCB.

The solder paste is a greyish substance consisting of tiny balls of metal, also known as solder. The solder paste mixes solder with a flux, which is a chemical designed help the solder melt and bond to a surface. Solder paste appears as a grey paste and must be applied to the board at exactly the right places and in precisely the right amounts.

In a professional PCBA line, which is also called a SMT line, a mechanical fixture holds the PCB and solder stencil in place. An applicator places the solder paste on the intended areas in precise amounts. The machine spreads the paste across the stencil, applying it evenly to every open area. After removing the stencil, the solder paste remains in the intended locations or the component pads.

Pick and Place

After applying the solder paste to the PCB board, the PCBA process moves on to the pick-and-place machine, a robotic device that places surface mount components, or SMDs, on a prepared PCB. SMDs account for most non-connector components on PCBs today. These SMDs are soldered onto the surface of the board in the next step of the PCBA process.

Traditionally, this was a manual process done with a pair of tweezers, in which rework technicians had to pick and place components by hand. This step is now an automated process among all the PCB manufacturers these days. This shift occurred largely because machines tend to be more accurate and more consistent than humans.

The device starts the pick-and-place process by picking up a PCB board with a vacuum grip and moving it to the pick-and-place station. The robot orients the PCB at the station and begins applying the SMTs to the PCB surface. These components are placed on top of the soldering paste in preprogrammed locations.

Reflow Soldering

Once the solder paste and surface mount components are all in place, they need to remain there. This means the solder paste needs to solidify, adhering the components to the board. The PCB assembly accomplishes this through a process called reflow.

Once the pick-and-place process concludes, the PCB board is transferred to a conveyor belt. This conveyor belt moves through a large reflow oven, which is somewhat like a commercial pizza oven. This oven consists of a series of heaters which gradually heat the board to a temperature around 250 degrees Celsius, or 480 degrees Fahrenheit. This is hot enough to melt the solder in the solder paste.

Once the solder melts, the PCB continues to move through the oven. It passes through a series of cooler heaters, which allow the melted solder to cool and solidify in a controlled manner. This creates a permanent solder joint to connect the SMDs to the PCB.

Many PCBAs require special consideration during reflow, especially for a two-sided PCB assembly. A two-sided PCB assembly needs stenciling and reflowing for each side separately. First, the side with fewer and smaller parts is stenciled, placed, and reflowed, followed by the other side.

Inspection and Quality Control

Once the surface mount components are soldered in place after the reflow process, as a next step the assembled board needs to be tested for functionality. Often, movement during the reflow process will result in poor connection quality or a complete lack of a connection. Shorts are also a common side effect of this movement, as misplaced components can sometimes connect portions of the circuit that should not connect.

Checking for these errors and misalignments can involve one of several different inspection methods. The most common inspection methods include manual, automatic, and X-ray check.

Manual Checks

Despite the upcoming development trend of automated and smart manufacturing, manual checks are still relied upon in the PCB assembly process. For smaller batches, an in-person visual inspection by a designer is an effective method to ensure the quality of a PCB after the reflow process. However, this method becomes increasingly impractical and inaccurate as the number of inspected boards increases. Looking at such small components for more than an hour can lead to optical fatigue, resulting in less accurate inspections.

Automatic Checks

Automatic optical inspection is a more appropriate inspection method for larger batches of PCBAs. An automatic optical inspection machine, also known as an AOI machine, uses a series of high-powered cameras to "see" PCBs. These cameras are arranged at different angles to view solder connections. Different quality solder connections reflect light in different ways, allowing the AOI to recognize a lower-quality solder. The AOI does this at a very high speed, allowing it to process a high quantity of PCBs in a relatively short time.

X-Ray Check

Another method of inspection involves X-rays. This is a less common inspection method. It's used most often for more complex or layered PCBs. The X-ray allows a viewer to see through layers and visualize lower layers to identify any potentially hidden problems.

After all these checks, the fate of a malfunctioning board depends on the PCBA company's standards; they will be sent back to be cleared and reworked, or scrapped.

Whether an inspection finds one of these mistakes or not, the next step of the process is to test the part to make sure it does what it's supposed to do. This involves testing the PCB connections for quality. Boards requiring programming or calibration require even more steps to test proper functionality.

Such inspections can occur regularly after the reflow process to identify any potential problems. These regular checks can ensure that errors are found and fixed as soon as possible, which helps both the manufacturer and the designer save time, labor, and materials.

Through Hole Assembly Process

PCBs with more electrical interconnects and mechanical components include through hole connectors beyond the usual SMDs. Drone boards are very good example and have an equal number of SMDs and through hole components. These can be plated through hole components or non-plated through hole components.

A plated through hole is a hole in the PCB that is plated all the way through the board. PCB components use these holes to pass a signal from one side of the board to the other. In this case, soldering paste will not do any good, as the paste will run straight through the hole without a chance to adhere.

Instead of soldering paste, PTH components require a more specialized kind of soldering method in the later PCB assembly process.

Manual Soldering

Manual through hole insertion is a straightforward process. Typically, one person at a single station is tasked with inserting one component into a designated PTH. Once they are finished, the board is transferred to the next station, where another person works on inserting a different component. The cycle continues for each PTH that needs to be outfitted. This can be a lengthy process, depending on how many PTH components need to be inserted during one cycle of the PCBA. Most companies specifically try to avoid designing with PTH components for this very purpose, but PTH components are still common among PCB designs.

Wave Soldering

Wave soldering is the automated version of manual soldering, but involves a very different process. Once the PTH component is put in place, the board is put on yet another conveyor belt. This time, the conveyor belt runs through a specialized oven where a wave of molten solder washes over the bottom of the board. This solders all of the pins on the bottom of the board at once. This kind of soldering is nearly impossible for double-sided PCBs, as soldering the entire PCB side would render any delicate electronic components useless.

After this soldering process is finished, the PCB can move to the final inspection, or it can run through the previous steps if the PCB needs additional parts added or another side assembled.

Final Inspection and Functional Test

After the soldering step of the PCBA process is finished, a final inspection will test the PCB for its functionality. This inspection is known as a functional test. The test puts the PCB through its paces, simulating the normal circumstances in which the PCB will operate. Power and simulated signals run through the PCB in this test while testers monitor the PCB's electrical characteristics.

If any of these characteristics, including voltage, current, or signal output, show unacceptable fluctuation or hit peaks outside of a predetermined range, the PCB fails the test. The failed PCB can then be recycled or scrapped, depending on the company's standards.

Testing is the final and most important step in the PCB assembly process since it determines the success or failure of the process. This is also the reason why regular testing and inspection throughout the assembly process is so important.

Post Process

Soldering paste leaves behind some amount of flux, while human handling can transfer oils and dirt from fingers and clothing to the PCB surface. Once all is done, the results can look a little unclean, which is both an aesthetic and a practical issue.

After months of remaining on a PCB, flux residue starts to smell and feel sticky. It also becomes somewhat acidic, which can damage solder joints over time. Additionally, customer satisfaction tends to suffer when shipments of new PCBs are covered in residue and fingerprints. For these reasons, washing the product after finishing all the soldering steps is important.

A stainless steel, high-pressure washing apparatus using deionized water is the best tool for removing residue from PCBs. Washing PCBs in deionized water poses no threat to the device. This is because it's the ions in regular water that do damage to a circuit, not the water itself. Deionized water, therefore, is harmless to PCBs as they undergo a wash cycle.

After washing, a quick drying cycle with compressed air leaves the finished PCBs ready for power-on.

Typically, the design engineers will be present at the factory to do the initial power-on. The factory power-on helps the engineers to fix any assembly-related issues in the factory itself. The skilled staff and the trained rework technicians can do the reworks at the same quality level as the machines.

Board Power-On

Once the PCBA is completed, there are several key preliminary and sanity checks to be done to ensure the board is ready for power-on. Powering on the board without finishing these steps can spoil the board, and there's a chance that the board can go dead and never become usable. This is why sanity tests are important; otherwise the efforts of many engineers to get a PCBA working will be in vain. A board can look like it works, but actually can have multiple hidden hardware issues that only pop up later when developing firmware/software, making the issues very difficult to debug. This is because the many independent subsystems communicate with each other and work together for complete functionality.

There is a large variation of possible things to check. They must be done very carefully and all observations must be captured so they can be revisited in case of any issues. The traditional checks before powering on a PCBA are elaborated below.

Basic Inspection

The first step is to check that all of the components used on the top and bottom layers are soldered as per BOM. Assembly is strictly as per install or no-install components in the production BOM.

No-install components are the optional components used in the design; they're not required for the power-on or basic functionality. This is usually for future scaling or backup circuits for secondary features.

All of the components should be verified for the manufacturing part numbers. Manufacturing part numbers should match exactly as given in the BOM, including the version ID and date code if any.

The pin 1 marking or orientation should match with the assembly file or the board file released along with the design package to the PCBA manufacturer.

Polarity of the discrete components should be verified as per the design. Installing polarized components like diodes, capacitors, and inductors in reverse can lead to shorts or component damage.

There should not be any visible short circuits between pads upon visual inspection. The pads should be soldered with good quality (QFN pads, connectors with a small pitch). High-end microscopes can check smaller size components clearly.

Short-Circuit Checks

After completing the sanity check, the board has to be verified for impedance and shorts. All the power rail points should be measured for impedance with respect to ground and other power rails. There must

151

not be any short (0 ohm resistance) between the power-to-power and power-to-ground connections.

Some power rails have very low impedance. The CPU core voltage of the latest generation processors from Intel with multiple cores can even show 1 ohm impedance due to the high current requirement for that rail. Some power rails may show low impedances like 20 ohms, 40 ohms, or 90 ohms due to higher current consumption.

Impedance of all the power rails should match the requirement before power-on. For example, all power rails shown in Figure 2-10 in Chapter 2 should show finite resistance when measured with a digital multimeter, which qualifies the board for safe power-on.

Power Check

If all the rail impedance is as expected or calculated, the next step is to connect the main input power to the board as per the main input power requirement. If the system is battery powered, it gets connected to a fully charged battery. Typically, a bench-top power supply with a digital display (for current and voltage) is used to feed power through the battery connectors to know the total current consumption of the board. This lets the test engineer limit the input current to the board to avoid any high current intake or system damage in case of any short.

The latest generation of SOCs categorize the rails for power and energy management. The always-on rails must be on at all the time, irrespective of the power state. A few rails may not be required by default; they will be available only when the appropriate software/firmware is installed. As a first step, always-on rails are verified on the board.

For example, in a drone system, the power for the propellers can be off when system is idle and grounded. It can be switched on when the system needs to take off when the application starts. This will save some power and protects the battery from draining. These rails are completely dependent on the software or application.

When the required input power is supplied to the board, the always-on power supply comes up. These power rail voltages should pass the voltage level and tolerance criteria as per the requirement.

For other voltages to come up, firmware or software needs to installed, which is the next step of the bring-up process. Power supplies that don't pass the exit criteria may have issues on the actual design, assembly, or even PCB.

A digital multimeter is suitable equipment to measure the power rails.

Sequencing and Reset Check

Power sequencing is an important feature to be tested, if all the power rails are as expected and meet the required tolerance. As explained in the previous chapter, every device needs specific power sequencing. The overall power sequencing is designed by consolidating all the individual device power sequencing requirements.

A multiple channel cathode ray oscilloscope (CRO) is the suitable equipment to check the power sequencing. Latest generation CROs support four channels simultaneously. Four rails can be connected together and the timings between those rails can be measured.

A high bandwidth CRO is required to measure the faster ramp timings and the very minute delays between power signals. Typically, there are individual enable and rest signals for different devices. All of them are control signals to be measured along with the power rails. A platform reset signal is the last signal released at the end of any power sequencing, which is usually released from the last power device to the SOC, after which the entire platform comes out of reset.

Figure 2-11 is an example of a power sequencing requirement. The timings on the actual board can be measured by probing the signals using a CRO. Capturing any two signals are enough to check the timings. Four signals are captured at the same time using a CRO, or a single logical analyzer is used to capture all of the signals at the same time.

Board-Level Testing

Software installation is the next stage if the board is electrically stable with the power supply, reset, and clocks. It's also ready for board-level functionality testing if all of the required software is in place.

The BIOS is the first-level software, which is flashed on the board immediately after power-on. In some designs, the BIOS is mandatory to complete the power sequencing, due to the software dependency of a few or more power rails. BIOS installation is followed by operating system installation and then the applications. Only after the BIOS, OS, and applications load will the board show all the power rails and any sign of operation. Without the software, none of the subsystems and input and output devices will work.

BIOS Flash Programming

The BIOS can be flashed in two ways in any system. Generally, there is a flash memory device on the board, which is usually nonvolatile memory of limited size to program the BIOS. The flash device can be programmed directly through an external connector on board, using a flash programmer. Alternately, the board can be connected to the host system through any communication interfaces to flash or update the BIOS through the command-line interface.

The flash program is usually a binary file, which only the host system understands. Typically, the size of the memory device and the BIOS file will be evaluated before the start of the project by the BIOS engineers.

In order to update the BIOS, the flash chip must be completely erased and updated with a flash programmer utility software. This is essentially the process known as "flashing the BIOS." This is referred to as "flashing" because the BIOS code is stored in flash memory.

Hardware settings and configurations can also be done in the BIOS using commands.

OS and Application Installation

An embedded operating system is typically designed to be resource-efficient and reliable. Resource efficiency comes at a cost of losing some functionality or granularity that larger computer operating systems provide, including functions that may not be used by the specialized applications they run. Depending on the method used for multitasking, this type of OS is frequently considered to be a real-time operating system (RTOS).

The drone works on the same operating system as any other embedded electronics system works. However, applications are customized and specifically built for the quadcopter. On top of the OS, web and mobile applications need to be customized for the drone.

For the Crop Squad drone, there are applications such as live image capture and analysis; also, connectivity needs to be developed, along with the drivers for the corresponding ingredients and subsystems to be developed.

Once the OS and the required applications are in place, the drone is ready for a board-level functionality check. A few of the system-level parts like the motor, camera, WiFi+BT, and LEDs can be directly wired to the board without mechanical interconnects to complete the board-level testing. This will validate all of the electrical ingredients in the PCB manufacturing factory itself, to avoid a board debug later after the PCBA moves away from the factory to the validation lab.

Functionality Check

The proper operation of the drone parts (system components) is important for smooth, safe flight and other operations. As a first-level test, drone hardware can be tested standalone with only a board-level assembly, without any mechanical structures assembled to validate all the board-level features. A board functionality check can be done after installing the OS and the required applications on the hardware.

In a typical Crop Squad drone architecture, there are numerous board-level components available to test the board functionality alone. The motherboard (`includes subsystems like SOC, memory, storage, flight controller, sensors`), daughterboard (`WiFi+BT module`), camera, battery, antenna, and motors are assembled first with all the electrical interconnects, without enclosures, to do the board-level functionality check.

The complete board-level validation helps the designers and test engineers fix any hardware or software level issues on the board before the system assembly. Hardware-level errors can be fixed by doing the rework on the PCBA, before putting it into the enclosure. If there are issues that can't be fixed by a rework, the board will go through the complete design cycle again. Board respins delay the product launch further and deviate the project from the original schedule. Apart from actual design issues, other hardware issues are unlikely if the hardware meets all the initial software requirements. Unlike hardware, software issues can be fixed easily at a later stage without doing any hardware rework.

If the hardware, software, and required applications are functionally verified, then a limited number of boards will be built and passed for software validation. The completion of the board and system validation qualifies the board for deployment.

Design Validation Testing

Design validation testing is done for the boards in any system to make sure the design is suitable for production. This process identifies any issues on the board. Issues can be identified anywhere in the design and can be on the basis of functionality, stress, or extreme corner case tests. Even if there are no issues, there might be opportunities for optimization, cost cutting, and yield increase in the next revision of boards or the next version of the product.

For hardware, the two critical validation processes are required to qualify the hardware for mass production. They are power and electrical validation testing. This validation enables the product for end user deployment.

Power Validation

Power validation is a must-do for each individual power supply design and also for the overall system power of drone. These power supplies are tested for various use case scenarios, operating conditions, and corner cases (for example, normal operating voltage at ambient, high, and low temperatures; high operating voltage at a low temperature; and low operating voltage at a higher temperature). All the validation test cases are done from the deployment perspective.

Validating the power supplies and verifying the performance for design margins is necessary to ensure a high quality and reliable product. Not verifying a power supply leaves a design vulnerable to a potentially unpleasant situation if problems arise after products are in the field. The product owner will have to recall or replace them with good working products. The manufacturer will incur a great loss if this happens. Some power supplies devices may operate without any issues under typical conditions, but may be at the edge of normal operation. When a power supply is heated or cooled, or when components age, its characteristics change to a point where a marginal design might fail.

No matter how basic a power supply may be, it should be tested by a qualified individual to ensure it meets system requirements. Irrespective of full software coding and full functionality verification, it is critical that the power supply be verified for proper working and operation with sufficient design margins.

A good understanding of various test cases, processes to perform, and data capturing can help do this effectively. A designer should establish a test specification and a test plan for the power supply. The test

157

specification should include all acceptable operating limits and the various operating conditions (`temperature, line conditions, and so forth`) under which the system must operate. A test plan describes the process of how to ensure the design meets the test specification.

System conditions (`line, loads, etc.`) and the environment vary greatly from application to application. Therefore, specific test specifications and plans vary from one system to another.

A bench-top power supply, an electronic load, a multimeter, an oscilloscope, and a network analyzer are required equipment for power validation testing.

Power Integrity

The primary step in validating any power supply is measuring the ripple, noise, and transients on the voltage rails. If issues are found for any power supply or if values are not within specified limits, the power supply need to be tuned until these values are within limits and to make the output clean.

There is no universally accepted method for measuring ripple and noise. Each manufacture, and sometimes different products from the same manufacturer, may have varying methods for these measurements. In some cases, the bandwidth of the test oscilloscope is defined as 20MHz or 100MHz. In addition, added components such as capacitors, resistors, twisted wires, and/or coax are sometimes required in the test setups that are defined by the manufacturer. In order to meet the product's specified ripple and noise specs, care must be taken to follow the manufacture's defined test setup.

Efficiency

Efficiency measurement is very important activity to be done for any power device, specifically battery operated systems. Low efficiency or unwanted power dissipation on any power supply may lead to unnecessary draining of the battery during normal operations.

The three basic pieces of equipment required to measure the efficiency are a programmable bench-top power supply, an electronic load, and digital multimeter.

Isolate the input and output connections for each power supply on the board. Supply the power from the bench-top power supply through input test points of the power devices on the board and connect the electronic load at the output of the power device. Measure input voltage, input current, output voltage, and output current for different load conditions. The product of the input voltage and input current will give input power similarly for output power. Apply the simple formula of Efficiency = Output Power/Input Power for every power supply rail used on the board.

Theoretical calculations may vary with the test results for few rails or sometimes all the rails. The differences need to be analyzed and calculations need to be corrected. Any issues in the efficiency need to be tuned to meet the target system power consumption as specified in the PRD.

Thermal

All the power devices and discrete components (`mosfet, power inductor, and bulk capacitors`) should be operated below the specified operating conditions for safe and reliable performance. Every component datasheet specifies the recommended operating temperature conditions. As seen in the earlier chapters, any component operating beyond the safe operating conditions shows a high failure rate and low reliability.

All of the critical or high power dissipating devices' case temperatures can be measured using a thermocouple. In addition to the ambient temperature, this testing has to be carried out under high and low operating temperature as well for consumer or industrial grades. Generally, the board is kept inside a thermal chamber in a higher load use case, with all of the board's cooling system in place (which is part of the `system assembly`). Each device is attached to the thermocouple with a longer wire extended outside of the chamber for measurement.

The temperature of the device is measured with different loads and use cases to make sure the package temperature is within the limits and complies with the latest international standards, such as the `JEDEC` `standard`. This will qualify the board as ready for deployment from the thermal perspective.

Power and Performance

One of the key factors of success for any product is meeting the power targets. The product features list the battery life for different use cases. Each system use case has specific power targets.

The system power targets are broken down to device-level power targets. Each device has its own power target. The active and standby power consumption of the system are calculated by putting down the active and standby power consumption of each device. The target power consumption values of each device are specified in the datasheet.

There is special equipment available to do this power measurement. For example, NIDAQ is data acquisition (DAQ) equipment to measure an electrical or physical phenomenon such as voltage, current, temperature, pressure, or sound with a computer.

This equipment supports multiple channel measurements at the same time. All the voltage rails can be connected simultaneously in the available channels along with the main system channel for current and voltage measurement. The high accurate data acquisition can be done for different system use cases like flight mode, active mode, and standby mode. Each subsystem's power consumption and the overall system power consumption are calculated from the acquisition results. The different levels of power consumption are correlated with the power targets specified in the PRD. The board and the system are considered ready if all the power targets are met. Any power supply that doesn't meet the power target needs to be relooked or redesigned. If it cannot be resolved due to a bug in the device or semiconductor itself, then the battery life time claimed in the PRD has to be revisited or changed according to the actual measurement.

Electrical Validation

Electrical validation captures the quality of the electrical signals for all of the subsystems. For example, interfaces like PCIe, SATA, and SD card between the SOC and the subsystems, as shown in the architecture block diagram, are verified for quality and reliability for all the test scenarios that qualify a drone as a product under various operating conditions. Similar to the power validation, electrical validation is also done from a product deployment perspective.

For both power and electrical validation testing, a detailed plan must be in place and agreed upon by all during the design phase itself.

Signal Integrity Testing

Signal integrity is a set of measurements to assess the quality of electrical signals. Electrical signals are simply a voltage or current waveform. All interfaces used on the system need to be verified and results must be captured.

Different probing techniques are used for singled ended and differential signals. The other categorizations are low speed and high speed signals. There is no clear distinction between low speed and high speed signals. Normally, frequencies beyond 50MHz signals are considered high speed signals. This also depends on the signal routing. Low frequency signals routed with longer lengths are also considered critical from the signal integrity.

161

Theoretically, although the design follows all the electrical constraints mentioned in Chapter 4, the physical board can have issues due to the variation in the calculated parameters and properties of the materials.

In a normally working board, the key parameters to be captured to validate the signal quality are signal frequency, overshoot, undershoot, rise time, fall time, and pulse width/shape from the quality perspective.

From the timing perspective, setup time and hold time between clock and data, for both read and write operations, must be captured and verified.

If these parameters meet the exit criteria and the values are well within the spec, then the board is declared deployment-ready.

Any of the measured values don't meet the spec, the issue must be fixed by hardware or software tuning. If any of the issues can't be fixed, the board will go through redesign cycle.

Most of the signal integrity issues occur due to the PCB trace impedance mismatch, return loss, insertion loss, cross talk, and jitter.

Optional circuits can be implemented on the design anticipating potential issues or if the designer is not confident enough about a particular interface. Optional circuits can be used for tuning if the designers anticipate any potential issues during the testing phase. This tuning can be done on the board at later time during the validation phase.

Integration Testing

Integration testing is completely software dependent. All the programmable ICs have to be installed with the right version of software to carry out this test. Integration testing test cases check that the overall interaction between different system components is happening as per specification. For example, single device read, single device write, interrupt read, interrupt service, device reset, and GPIO enable/disable are part of integration testing.

Drone Assembly

In the previous sections, we discussed the generic flow of a system assembly, bring-up, and validation. In the following sections, we will discuss how the generic flow applies to the drone product life cycle.

All of the drone parts play key roles in the proper flight. Each and every part needs to be validated against the design. No drone part is insignificant; even the screws must fit properly, without any tolerance mismatch, for a smooth and safe flight.

Knowledge of each part is important before assembling the drone and help in case of debugging any issues with the flight. The following is the list of key drone parts to be assembled for the complete system. Most of the system parts, other than the board, are buy items. They can be standard parts or customized parts purchased from third-party vendors.

- Propellers

- Motors

- Landing gear

- Drone enclosures

- Drone hardware

Drone System Validation Testing

Drone system validation includes a broad range of checks from the visual inspection to flight observation and functionality check. Each mechanical part of the drone has a checklist to be verified before assembly.

Propellers are responsible for pulling the drones into the air from the ground and pushing it forward. Most consumer drone propellers are made from plastic or carbon fiber. Measure the length, width, thickness, and shape of the propeller if it is manufactured as per the design requirement.

Motor design is very important for a drone. The selection of more efficient, more reliable, and quieter motors is key. More efficient motors save battery life.

For a drone, some of the key system-level test cases are

- Drone idle mode

- Drone flight mode

- WIFI+BT communication

- Wireless remote control

- Battery charging and discharging

- Still capture ground and flight

- Video capture ground and flight

System Pilot Build

After completing the system validation testing, with all of the quality and reliability criteria passed, the drone can be declared deployment-ready. If the system is deployment-ready, manufactures will use their high volume manufacturing techniques to do the pilot builds.

Factory tooling is done to automate certain production tasks in a common high volume manufacturing tasks. Assembly lines are one good example of high volume manufacturing areas where components are put together piece-by-piece by human workers, machines, or a combination of the two. Each worker or machine in the assembly performs a specific task and then passes a unit onto another worker or machine until all the tasks necessary to create a final product are performed. Factory workers are often trained by the mechanical engineer via assembly instructions to assemble the final drone product.

Pilot builds are distributed to limited internal customers for product testing. These pilot builds are tested only in a lab environment. A few samples of the pilot builds are supplied for product certification. The pilot builds can be distributed for field testing only after certification by an authorized regulatory test lab.

Summary

How a bunch of software design package files transforms into a complete, physical PCBA, through the PCB fabrication and assembly process, is what this chapter is all about.

The completed PCBA or hardware then comes back to designer's hands for testing and validation. The detailed validation and verification checks the hardware for quality, reliability, and deployment readiness. Hardware, after meeting the criteria, qualifies for drone system assembly. The drone is validated again as a product for deployment readiness, with all the preplanned system-level tests. The positive results from the system-level testing triggers the pilot build at the factory. The pilot build is just the beginning (it's also called pre-production units). This contributes to the fine tuning of hardware and software. After all this, the final step to take the system to production is certification.

CHAPTER 6

Software Development

In general, for any system design, the first step is to do the hardware and software partitioning, meaning identifying what goes in the hardware and what goes in the software. The hardware design part was addressed in the earlier chapters.

In the chapters so far, we have discussed the drone system design from hardware perspective, which is the primary objective of the book. In this chapter, now, we will cover the software aspect of the system. The chapter title may not be a great fit since the chapter will not only cover the software development, but will start from the planning and cover the development, integration, and maintenance of the same.

The majority of the software development process and consideration will be similar to any standard software development, which is covered in many books and other material. The key focus in this chapter, therefore, will be to address the drone-specific aspects of software design. There are two such factors: low power and the real-time aspect.

Software Development and Deployment

Software development and deployment is a detailed process consisting of many phases. The overall process flow is called software development life cycle.

© Neeraj Kumar Singh, Porselvan Muthukrishnan, Satyanarayana Sanpini 2019
N. K. Singh et al., *Industrial System Engineering for Drones*,
https://doi.org/10.1007/978-1-4842-3534-8_6

Software Development Life Cycle

The software development life cycle (SDLC) is the process of planning, implementing, testing, deploying, and maintaining a software system. In this context, there are multiple pieces of software that need to be developed and then integrated to create a platform and then validated for the right functionality and then debugged in case of issues and then maintained and upgraded as necessary.

So, overall, the stages or steps that apply to the drone software design and deployment are as follows:

- Development

- Integration

- Validation

- Debug

- Maintenance

In our drone design, a lot of software will be procured from different vendors and only a part of the whole software stack will be developed in-house.

As far as development is concerned, there are multiple stages involved in the development itself: preliminary analysis, system analysis, system design, and implementation. In our particular case, a majority of the software components will be provided by the component supplier, so the real activities will start with integration. However, there are still some components that need to be developed in-house.

In the software development business, various activities relating to the development through maintenance follow specific processes and methodologies. These processes and methodologies put together define a model. In the next few sections, we'll talk about some of the most prominent models and choose the specific model to employ.

Software Development Models

There are various software development models in practice. By model we mean various processes and methodologies that we apply during software development. The models are chosen based on the nature of the software project, meaning certain models are more suited for specific kinds of projects. The following sections cover a few of the more prominent software development models in practice.

Waterfall Model

The waterfall model follows the sequential approach where each key activity in the process is represented as a separate phase and carried out one after another. In other words, in the waterfall model, phases like requirements, design, implementation, testing, and maintenance are carried out one after another. Therefore, for example, the design will not start until all requirements have been captured and analyzed. Figure 6-1 illustrates the waterfall model.

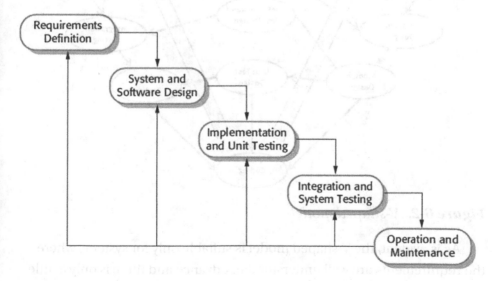

Figure 6-1. *Waterfall model*

As might be evident, the waterfall method is most suited for systems where the requirements are well understood in advance and there is little chance of any change.

V-Shaped Model

The V-shaped software development model is similar to the waterfall model in the sense that execution of the processes happen in a sequential manner; however, it's in a V-shape. V-shaped SDLC is also called a verification and validation model since it is driven by the testing/verification/validation at each of the development phases. Figure 6-2 illustrates the V-shaped model in detail.

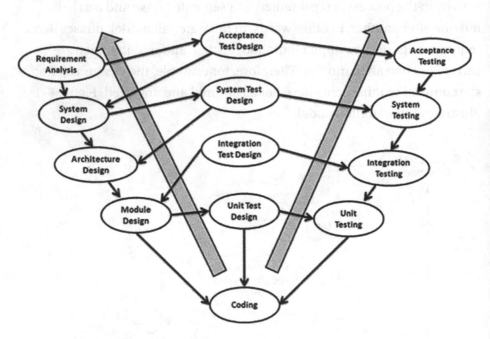

Figure 6-2. *V-shaped model*

As is evident, the V-shaped model is suitable only for systems where the requirements are well understood in advance and there is only a little chance of a change in the requirements.

Incremental, Iterative, and Agile

Incremental, iterative, and agile are slightly different but related models.

The incremental model develops an initial implementation, exposes the same to a user for feedback, and takes it through several versions until the complete system has been developed.

The iterative development model aims to develop a system through building small portions of all the features, across all components.

So, the key difference between the incremental methodology and the iterative methodology is that each increment in the incremental approach builds a complete feature of the software, while in the iterative approach, it builds small portions of all the features. In other words, in a sense, during iterative development model, only the implementation part is taken in iterations while the feature set of the product remain the same; however, during the incremental development phase, the feature set changes from version to version.

The agile development methodology, in a way, combines the two models, incremental and iterative. In the agile methodology, there are iterations of predefined periods/timelines. The iterative approach is taken and working software is delivered after each iteration. Each build is incremental in terms of the features set; the final build holds all the features required for the system. Figure 6-3 illustrates the agile model.

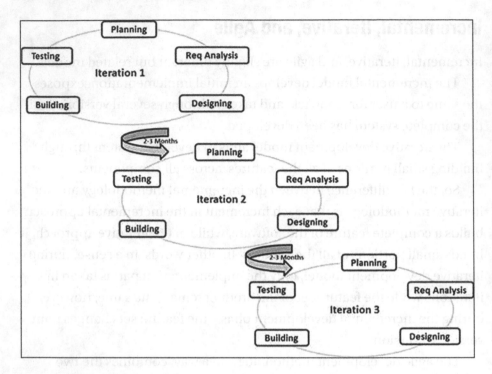

Figure 6-3. *Agile model*

As might be evident, the incremental, iterative, and agile methodologies are most suited for systems where the final feature set is not known in advance (depends upon the customer feedback) and/or the feature set/priority of specific features might change, which is usually the case for most software systems today. It is therefore easy to extrapolate that these methodologies are very common and prevalent today.

This discussion gives a quick summary of the most common methodologies in use. They are not the only models. Other models like the RAD (rapid application development) model and the spiral model are not so common. Bringing the discussion back to our drone design, our requirements are fairly well known in advance, and it not feasible to test the drone at the system level with half-baked/partial features. Therefore, for our system, we'll use the waterfall methodology.

Having discussed the key processes, methodologies, and models in the software development and deployment, let's talk about what software components we require, what specific design and development considerations need to be applied, what methodologies/models we apply for each of them, and finally how these components integrate. Let's start with the software stack of a generic system and then move to the specifics.

Software Stack

A software stack is a set of software subsystems or components needed to create a complete platform. In addition to the components set/list, a software stack also refers to the inter-relationship of these components. A typical software stack looks like Figure 6-4.

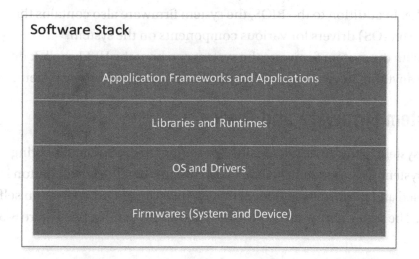

Figure 6-4. *Software Stack*

Figure 6-4 shows the software components logically organized as layers. At the bottom is the firmware component, which can be considered as part of the hardware as well. The layer above is for the OS and drivers, which are considered the privileged software and can access the hardware and resources that the upper layers (libraries/runtime and applications) cannot. This boundary is commonly referred to as the kernel mode and user mode of operation.

Hardware

Since the system software depends a lot on the underlying hardware, let's recap the hardware design of our reference drone. At the center is a SoC, which acts as the central point and glues everything together. Then there are various discrete hardware components that are connected to the SoC via various controller interfaces, such as a camera, sensors (including GPS), connectivity (WiFi+BT), a charger, and so on.

Now, from the software perspective, first we need the system firmware, which boots the system up. The system firmware is provided by the SoC vendor. In addition to the BIOS, the system firmware also contains the UEFI (pre-OS) drivers for various components on the system.

With the system firmware the system can boot the UEFI shell. It doesn't have anything to get to so now we need to install an OS on the system.

System Firmware and Device

The system firmware is responsible for setting up the SoC and booting the system. The system firmware takes charge when the power button is pressed and performs the boot activities, including POST (power on self-test). The system firmware is provided by the SoC vendor. See Figure 6-5.

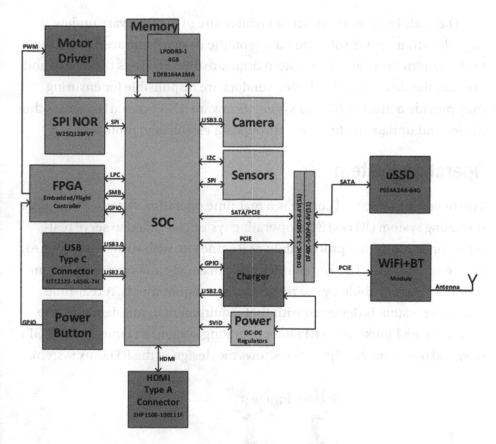

Figure 6-5. *Hardware design block diagram*

In today's world (systems), devices have firmware as well. The
device firmware, along with the device hardware, provides the specified
functionality. Typically, device firmware is part of the device itself. It is,
however, possible to upgrade device firmware (which is one of the key
reasons for having hardware and firmware as separate entities). There
are only few instances when we need to update the firmware of a device
already put into market. The device vendors provide proprietary tools and
mechanisms along with the updated firmware for upgrading the firmware.
The OS vendors create the standards for device firmware update capsule.

The high-level mechanism or architecture of the firmware update capsule is that the OS software passes on the device firmware as a payload to the system firmware. The system firmware then accesses the device and updates the firmware. The device vendors are responsible for ensuring they provide a mechanism for system firmware (UEFI-based) to access the device and update the firmware through an established protocol.

Operating System

The operating system of choice is a real-time operating system. A real-time operating system (RTOS) is an operating system intended to serve real-time applications that process data as it comes in, with stringent response time requirements. The key characteristic of a real-time operating system is that it needs to abide by the response time requirements. A real-time operating system is designed with that requirement in mind. In our case, we chose the Linux-based RTLinux operating system. RTLinux is GNU-GPL licensed open source. Figure 6-6 shows the design of the RTLinux system.

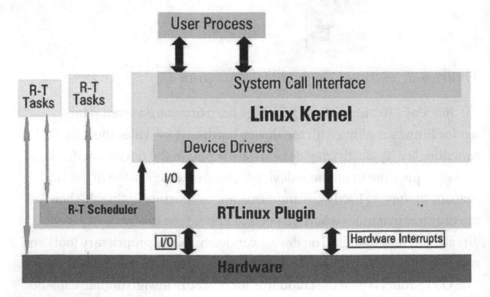

Figure 6-6. *RTLinux system architecture*

As can be seen, in the RTLinux operating system, there is a layer (the RTLinux layer or RTLinux plugin) between the real hardware and the standard Linux kernel.

The standard Linux kernel is not modified at all, and in a RTLinux operating system, the RTLinux plugin/layer takes over the overall scheduling and proxies to the standard kernel as the hardware. The Real-Time Tasks are directly handled by the RTLinux layer, while the standard kernel is treated as a low priority monolithic task.

The key things to note about the RTLinux layer or plugin:

- RTLinux sits between the real hardware and kernel.

- It acts as hardware for the Linux kernel.

- It treats the kernel as a monolithic big process.

RTLinux can be downloaded from the Web. It is open source, so we can customize the system as needed.

RTLinux Design

In order to understand the design of RTLinux, we need to understand the architecture and working of the standard Linux kernel. The Linux kernel separates the hardware from the user-level software and applications. The kernel is responsible for scheduling and assigning priority to each task in order to optimize the user experience and performance. The scheduling policy is a priority-based time sharing (FIFO, round robin, etc.) system, which implies that the kernel has the ability to suspend any task once it has consumed the time-slice allotted. This scheduling algorithm along with device drivers, uninterruptible system calls, interrupt disabling (at specific points), and virtual memory usage and operations, are the sources of unpredictability in terms of response time and performance of a task. After executing a task for a predetermined time-slice, the standard Linux kernel could preempt the task and schedule another one. Therefore, the continuity of the task gets lost. If the task doesn't have a real-time

177

requirement, the task might not realize it since all this switching back and forth happens very quickly. However, the fact of the matter is that in trying to ensure fair distribution of CPU time among all tasks, the kernel can prevent uninterrupted usage of the CPU by any one particular task.

Now, the fundamental expectation from a real-time kernel is that the kernel is able to guarantee the timing requirements of the running tasks. The RTLinux kernel accomplishes real-time performances by removing the sources of unpredictability just discussed. As we can see in Figure 6-6, we can consider the RTLinux kernel as sitting between the standard Linux kernel and the hardware. The RTLinux layer proxies as the hardware, and therefore, the Linux kernel sees the RTLinux layer as the actual hardware. The Linux kernel runs as yet another task, which runs along with other RT tasks. Now, the user can both introduce and set priorities to each and every task. The scheduling of Real-Time Tasks is handled by the RTLinux layer and not by the standard Linux kernel. The user can achieve correct timing for the processes by deciding on the scheduling algorithms, priorities, frequency of execution, and so on. The RTLinux layer assigns the lowest priority to the standard Linux kernel.

Another chance to accomplish the real-time performance is by intercepting all hardware interrupts: only for the interrupts relating to the Real-Time Tasks an appropriate interrupt service routine is run. All other interrupts are passed onto the Linux kernel as software interrupts. The standard Linux kernel runs when the RTLinux kernel is idle. The RTLinux executive itself is non-preemptible.

Yet another tweak to improve the real-time performance is Real-Time Tasks are privileged and therefore have direct access to the hardware, and they do not use virtual memory (virtual memory is one of the biggest causes of unpredictability). Real-time tasks are written as special Linux modules that can be dynamically loaded into memory. The initialization code for a Real-Time Task initializes the Real-Time Task structure and informs the RTLinux kernel of its deadline, period, and release-time constraints.

RTLinux coexists along with the Linux kernel since we don't need to modify the standard Linux kernel. As discussed, by applying some relatively simple modifications and tricks, RTLinux manages to convert the standard Linux kernel into a hard real-time operating system.

Having discussed the architecture and design of RTLinux, let's discuss the software stack/architecture of the overall drone system. With real-time Linux, a potential software architecture would look like Figure 6-7. The RTLinux kernel sits above the hardware. Real-time processes are handled by the RTLinux kernel/layer directly. The non-real-time processes are handled by the standard Linux kernel. The task named "Service Agent Task" in Figure 6-7 is a service listening and responding to the remote request (monitoring, control, etc.). The remote monitoring and control tasks connect to the "Service Agent Task" via the internet/network protocol.

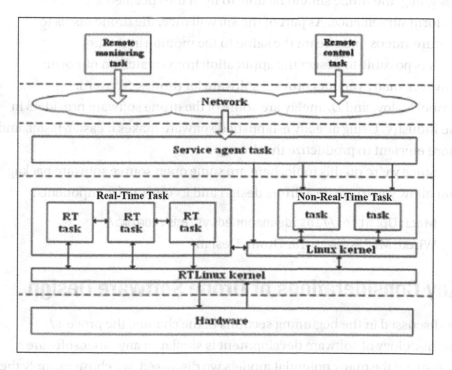

Figure 6-7. *Complete Software architecture with RTLinux*

SDK and Libraries

In general, there are many third-party SDKs and libraries available to procure, install, and use for our purposes. In this particular case, we need the Imaging SDKs for surveillance purposes. The OpenCV and GStreamer SDKs are good enough for our sample drone. OpenCV is a vision-related SDK that allows us to make sense of captured data. It allows us to identify the object in an image and take actions based on it, if needed. GStreamer is the media framework that allows us to capture and transform data.

Application

The application layer is responsible for accomplishing the intended purpose of the drone. There are two key elements of the system we are designing: the drone should be able to fly in the specified areas and perform surveillance. As part of the surveillance, the drone needs to capture videos and stream the same to the monitoring station.

It is possible to design the application from scratch on our own; however, many vendors provide software for drones. Skyward, DroneDeploy, and DroneFly are some of the drone software providers in the industry. Using already established software makes it easier, faster, and more efficient to productize the drone.

Since we're on this topic, here are some open source software packages that allow you to create a drone design and its essential components:

Mach Up: http://insideunmannedsystems.com/ma/
Wired: MIT Software for Drone Design

Key Considerations of Drone Software Design

As discussed in the beginning sections of the chapter, the process/ methodology of software development is similar to any other software system. Of the many potential models we discussed, we chose to apply the waterfall methodology since it suits our needs: the requirements are well known and it is of little use to provide a half-baked/partially featured drone to users for feedback/testing (as done in incremental/iterative model).

It is, however, evident that there are a few specific attributes of a drone system that requires consideration. These software design/development considerations are not isolated from the hardware design, therefore we shall discuss them in tandem. This means we will talk about the specific attributes of a drone system and follow that up with the specific design considerations in hardware and software in order to support the needs. The two key attributes that need consideration while designing a drone system are

1. Drones are battery-powered systems, meaning they should run for a while with one charge of battery. So we must optimize the power of the system by applying the low-power design rules/guidelines.

2. Drones are real-time systems, meaning that drones run under very stringent timing/response time constraints. Drones are flying devices that capture/ sense the data and they need to process the data and respond/react quickly in order to avoid potentially fatal events.

In the following sections, we will talk about both of these aspects in detail and discuss the specific hardware and software design choices we need to make.

Low Power

A drone runs on battery and needs to be power efficient to run for longer without requiring a recharge (of the battery). This is not to say that systems not running on batteries need not be power efficient. It is important to be power efficient all the time; however, it is all the more important for a battery-operated device to be more power efficient than ones always connected to power.

HW Considerations

At a system level, we need to manage the system power at all times, meaning when the system is active (active power management), when it is idle (idle power management), and also during connected standby (connected standby power management). There are many design considerations in order to manage power for all three scenarios; however, the key ones boil down to the following:

1. Components in the system should support different operating performance levels with respective power consumption levels. This allows for optimizing power by means of running at the appropriate performance levels. Since the higher performance level requires higher power and the lower performance level accordingly lower power, by setting the components to the appropriate performance level, the system is able to optimize power.

2. Components in the system should support various sleep states with differing wakeup latency: deeper sleep states consume less power, but have longer wakeup latency. Using the components' behavior, the system/software can set the idle components to the appropriate (based on wakeup latency) lower power sleep states and thereby save power.

3. The platform should support system-level lower power states: the software can put the system to the appropriate system-level power state by exercising/leveraging these states and thereby save power.

4. And, at the platform design level, the design choices
    should be made in such a way that the components
    involved in one use case share the power resources(or
    in other words, in the same power domain); however,
    more importantly, the components engaged in
    mutually exclusive usages should *not* be sharing the
    power resources. This enables the system/software to
    switch off the power resource for components not in
    use and thereby save power.

SW Considerations

In order to understand and appreciate the SW considerations better, we
ought to understand the fundamentals of power consumption, followed by
the philosophy applied to power saving or optimizations.

Power Consumption of a System

Roughly speaking, systems have two modes when powered on: the first is
the active mode when the system is actively being used and the second
mode is when the system is on but it's on standby and waiting for input
from the user. In the standby mode, to save power, most of the system
components can be turned off since they are idle. To effectively manage
the power and state transition, the Advanced Configuration and Power
Interface (ACPI) standard defines various system states and device states
in detail. Generally speaking, the device/IP is nonfunctional in low-power
states. In order to use the device/IP again, one needs to bring the device/
IP back to a functional state from the low-power, nonfunctional state. The
time taken in the process is called wake-up latency. Again, a general rule of
thumb is, the lower the power state, the longer it takes to bring the device/
IP to a fully functional state (the greater the wake-up latency).

So, speaking of the power consumed by a system, as shown in Figure 6-8, the total power consumed is a summation of active mode power consumption, standby (sleep) mode power consumption, and wake-up power. Wake-up power is the power wasted during wake-up. In a nutshell, there are three categories of power consumption as listed below and shown in Figure 6-8, and separate strategies are applied to optimize them in a system:

1. Power consumption in active mode

2. Power consumption in standby mode

3. Power wastage during system wake

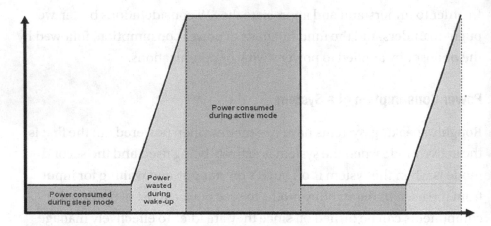

Figure 6-8. *Power consumption of a system across active, standby, and transit modes*

Power Optimization at the System Level

While discussing power optimization at the system level, we will discuss the optimization on three fronts: active power management, idle power management, and connected standby power management.

Active Power Management

Active power management refers to the management of power when the system is being used. The main thing to understand about APM is the fact that even when the system is in use, only a few of the subsystems are active; therefore, the rest of the system components can be turned off. To this end, the system is designed with use cases in mind, such that when a system is in use in a particular way, only the resources required for that use case are active and the rest can be power-gated to save maximum power.

Idle Power Management

Idle power management is the set of policies that are employed to save power when the system is idle. In modern systems, it is also desirable that the system is able to resume a normal full functional state as soon as there is need for it. The need may arise from an incoming call or the user's desire to wake the system for normal usage. The idle power management requires that the system is in a state where it consumes as little power as possible. However, the components must be able to become functional in very little time. To this end, there is a lot of effort on the part of the system designers, hardware IP designers, and OS designers.

Connected Standby Power Management

Modern systems are not only supposed to be using little power when idle and come back up to working state when required, but there is a third dimension to it. That is, even when idle, the system is connected to the world and keeps up to date with all that is happening. For example, the system keeps the stock tab, news, and social media notifications all up to date so that when a user opens it up, the user finds everything up to date. In addition, the system should be able to notify the user of the events the user has subscribed to. Towards this end, the whole system is designed in such a way that

1. System components (at least some) have a state where they consume very little power, all the functional parts are shut down, but they have a portion that is always on and connected.

2. The entry and exit to the low power state is limited and predictable.

3. *Offload*: System components have built-in intelligence such that they can function and do some basic jobs without involving other system components. For example, the network devices in a connected standby platform must be capable of protocol offloads. Specifically, the network device must be capable of offloading the Address Resolution Protocol (ARP), Name Solicitation (NS), and several other WiFi-specific protocols. And for another example, audio playback can be offloaded such that during audio playback only the audio controller is active and everybody else can go to low-power states (after setting things up for the audio controller, of course).

4. Wake: System components have a mechanism to wake the system when required. This occurs in three cases:

   4.1. One of the offloaded components has discovered some event for which it needs to involve other system components.

   4.2. One of the offloaded components needs assistance from another component to carry out further instructions.

4.3.   The user has requested the system to come up for action via any of the interfaces (typically buttons).

5.   The OS and software are designed in such a way that at every small interval the system comes up online, does routine housekeeping, updates the relevant tabs, and goes back to sleep. In this context, modern operating systems have introduced a new concept, time coalescing, which simply means that the recurring booking jobs are aligned such that the system is able to carry out all tasks in one wakeup instance and they don't require a separate wakeup for each of them, which would be counterproductive to say the least.

ACPI States

In order to facilitate optimal power management at the system level, ACPI has defined standard states for system, devices, processors, and so on. Figure 6-9 shows the various states defined by ACPI and the transitions between them. In the following sections, we talk about them and explain what they all mean.

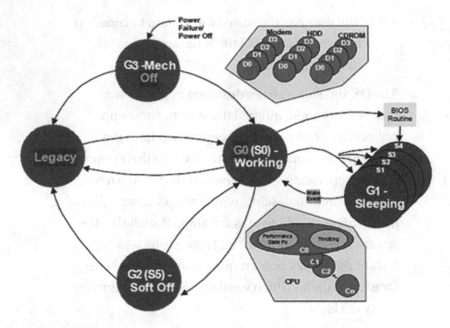

Figure 6-9. *Global system power states and transitions*

Global and System States

ACPI defines four global states and a total of six system states. The global states are marked G0–G3 while the system states are marked as S0–S5. It must be noted that even though S6 is mentioned in some motherboard documents, it is not an ACPI-defined state. S6, wherever mentioned, corresponds to G3.

ACPI defines a mechanism to transition the system between the working state (G0) and a sleeping state (G1) or the soft-off (G2) state. During transitions between the working and sleeping states, the context of the user's operating environment is maintained. ACPI defines the quality of the G1 sleeping state by defining the system attributes of four types of ACPI sleeping states (S1, S2, S3, and S4). Each sleeping state is defined to allow implementations that can trade off cost, power, and wake latencies.

1. G0/S0: In the G0 state, work is being performed by the OS/application software and the hardware. The CPU or any particular hardware device could be in any one of the defined power states (C0-C3 or D0-D3); however, some work will be taking place in the system.

   a. S0: The system is in a fully working state.

2. G1: In the G1 state, the system is assumed to be doing no work. Prior to entering the G1 state, the OSPM will place devices in a device power state compatible with the system sleeping state to be entered; if a device is enabled to wake the system, then the OSPM will place these devices into the lowest Dx state from which the device supports wake.

   a. S1: The S1 state is defined as a low wake-latency sleeping state. In this state, the entire system context is preserved with the exception of CPU caches. Before entering S1, the OSPM will flush the system caches.

   b. S2: The S2 state is defined as a low wake latency sleep state. This state is similar to the S1 sleeping state where any context except for system memory may be lost. Additionally, control starts from the processor's reset vector after the wake event.

   c. S3: Commonly referred to as standby, sleep, or suspend to RAM (STR), the S3 state is defined as a low wake-latency sleep state. From the software viewpoint, this state is functionally the same as the S2 state. The operational difference is that some power resources that may have been left on in the S2 state may not be available to the S3 state. As such, some devices may be in a lower power state when the system is in the S3 state than when the system is in the S2 state. Similarly, some device wake events can function in S2 but not S3.

d. S4: Also known as hibernation or suspend to disk, the S4 sleeping state is the lowest-power, longest wake-latency sleeping state supported by ACPI. In order to reduce power to a minimum, it is assumed that the hardware platform has powered off all devices. Because this is a sleeping state, the platform context is maintained. Depending on how the transition into the S4 sleeping state occurs, the responsibility for maintaining system context changes between the OSPM and BIOS. To preserve context, in this state all content of the main memory is saved to non-volatile memory such as a hard drive and is powered down. The contents of RAM are restored on resume. All hardware is in the off state and maintains no context.

3. G2/S5: Also referred as soft off. In G2/S5, all hardware is in the off state and maintains no context. The OSPM places the platform in the S5 soft off state to achieve a logical off. The S5 state is not a sleeping state (it is a G2 state) and no context is saved by the OSPM or hardware but power may

still be applied to parts of the platform in this state
and as such, it is not safe to disassemble. Also
from a hardware perspective, the S4 and S5 states
are nearly identical. When initiated, the hardware
will sequence the system to a state similar to the
off state. The hardware has no responsibility for
maintaining any system context (memory or I/O);
however, it does allow a transition to the S0 state
due to a power button press or a remote start.

4. G3: Also called mechanical off, G3 is the same as
    S5; additionally, the power supply is isolated. The
    computer's power has been totally removed via
    a mechanical switch and no electrical current is
    running through the circuitry, so it can be worked
    on without damaging the hardware.

Device States

In addition to global and system states, ACPI defines various device states
ranging from D0 to D3.

1. D0: This state is assumed to be the highest level of
    functionality and power consumption. The device is
    completely active and responsive, and is expected to
    remember all relevant contexts.

2. D1: The meaning of the D1 device state is defined
    by each device class. Many device classes may not
    define D1. In general, D1 is expected to save less
    power and preserve more device context than D2.
    Devices in D1 may cause the device to lose some
    context.

191

3. D2: The meaning of the D2 device state is defined by each device class. Many device classes may not define D2. In general, D2 is expected to save more power and preserve less device context than D1 or D0. Devices in D2 may cause the device to lose some context.

4. D3 Hot: The meaning of the D3 Hot state is defined by each device class. Devices in the D3 Hot state are required to be software enumerable. In general, D3 Hot is expected to save more power and optionally preserve device context. If device context is lost when this state is entered, the OS software will reinitialize the device when transitioning to D0.

5. D3 Cold: Power has been fully removed from the device. The device context is lost when this state is entered, so the OS software will reinitialize the device when powering it back on. Since device context and power are lost, devices in this state do not decode their address lines. Devices in this state have the longest restore times.

Processor States

ACPI defines the power state of system processors while in the G0 working state as being either active (executing) or sleeping (not executing). Processor power states are designated C0, C1, C2, C3, ... Cn. The C0 power state is an active power state where the CPU executes instructions. The C1 through Cn power states are processor sleeping states where the processor consumes less power and dissipates less heat than leaving the processor in the C0 state. While in a sleeping state, the processor does not execute any instructions. Each processor's sleeping state has a latency associated with entering and exiting that corresponds to the power savings.

In general, the longer the entry/exit latency, the greater the power savings for the state. To conserve power, OSPM places the processor into one of its supported sleeping states when idle. While in the C0 state, ACPI allows the performance of the processor to be altered through a defined "throttling" process and through transitions into multiple performance states (P-states). A diagram of processor power states is provided in Figure 6-10.

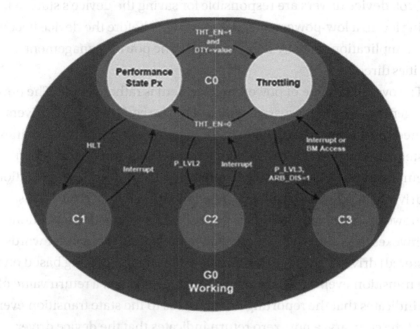

Figure 6-10. Processor power states

It is clear from the above discussion that detecting inactivity and putting the devices and eventually the system (if possible) in their low power states forms the heart of power management software.

Linux Power Management

In Linux, the power management software manages state transitions in association with device drivers and applications. It circulates the PM events, including standby state transitions and sleep state transitions, to various software components. This way the software components can participate in the state transitions decisions. For example, based on the situation, individual components can veto certain state transitions.

Since most of the devices have operating context or state, there is a need to save and restore the same as and when the devices transition into and out of the low power state. Based on the Linux power management protocol, device drivers are responsible for saving the device's state before putting it into a low-power state and restoring it before the device becomes active. Applications usually don't engage in the power management activities directly.

The overall scheme of power management is rather simple. The power management system discussed earlier plays the central role. All drivers that need and want to participate in the system state transition activities register with the power management system. The power management system maintains a list of all registered drivers. At the time of registration, the driver also provides a callback function for state transition events. The power management system is aware of the system state transitions and invokes the callback function of all participating (or in other words, registered) drivers. The callback function does the processing based on the state transition event type and returns an integer value: a return value of zero indicates that the reporting driver agrees to the state transition event, and at the contrary, a non-zero return indicates that the device driver doesn't agree to the state transition request. The nonzero return value causes the power management system to abort the state transition flow.

The callbacks are invoked in a predictable order. Based on the implementation, the driver that registers last is invoked first. Figure 6-11 illustrate the flow more visually. In this example, there are three drivers: A, B, and C. In the beginning, all three of them are in running/active state, as shown.

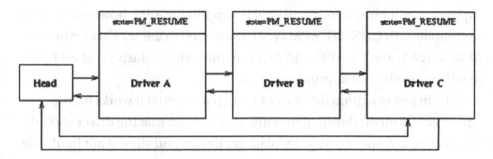

Figure 6-11. *System in running state*

Now, let's say the system wants to transition to a standby state. In order to achieve that, the PM system sends out a standby request to all three drivers, and assuming all three drivers agree to the transition, the system state now looks like Figure 6-12, wherein the devices have been put into a standby state.

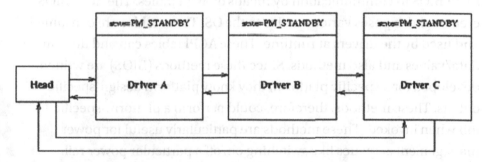

Figure 6-12. *System in standby state*

At the time of driver unload (say when the device is removed or something of that sort), the driver can call upon the PM system to indicate that it is not interested in participating in the PM events and wants to unregister. And, as expected, the PM system will not bother the driver (on state transitions) once it has unregistered itself from the PM system.

From the system power management perspective there are two models/protocols/specifications: APM and ACPI. APM is rather older than ACPI. ACPI is the specification most systems follow; however, APM is also supported on Linux. In order to enable support for APM, however, we need to compile with CONFIG_APM=y. Also, we need to tell bootloader to use APM instead of ACPI. APM and ACPI are mutually exclusive and we need to tell the bootloader appropriately.

The driver is written for devices in such a way that it works for the device across all platforms, generally. That implies that the driver should not assume any specific system/platform design and should not hardcode any values that will change from platform/system design to design. Drivers, however, might need some parameters that depend on the platform design. The information may be needed by the driver to make the device functional, or power management transitions, and so on.

The question is what mechanism should we apply to pass these specific parameters to the driver? The answer to this is ACPI, again. ACPI, as part of the specification, provides a mechanism for drivers and the ACPI BIOS to communication by means of ACPI tables. The ACPI BIOS creates and exposes various tables to the OS. These tables are consumed and used by the drivers at runtime. These ACPI tables can and do contain data/values and also methods. Since these methods (BIOS) are written/developed for a specific platform, they know platform design-specific details. These methods, therefore, could perform a platform-specific job when invoked. These methods are particularly useful for power management activities like switching on/off a particular power rail.

These ACPI methods are compiled into the AML (ACPI machine language) and interpreted (when invoked) by AMLI built into the OS. In addition to the mechanism to provide raw tables to the OS, the ACPI specification defines the device power state transition and management very meticulously. In order to support the power management flows, there are specific methods that are defined for predefined purposes. These predefined methods are invoked by the ACPI driver at a specific event. Some of the key methods are summarized as follows (the list is not supposed to be exhaustive, but for illustration purpose only):

1. _PRx: _PRx (where x could be 0, 1, 2, or 3, respective to each supported device state) methods specify what power resources are needed for the device to operate in state Dx. The ACPI framework in the OS needs to ensure that when the device transitions into Dx, power resources for the same are turned on. _PRx methods are defined in a particular device node scope and apply to that particular device.

2. _PSx: _PSx(where x could be 0,1,2, or 3, respective to each supported device state) methods are called when the device transitions to state Dx. _PSx is intended to perform any platform-specific actions required during these transitions. Similar to _PRx, _PSx methods are defined in a particular device node scope and apply to that particular device.

3. _SxW: On a given platform, there is a specific mapping between device states that supports the wake capability and system states that can respond to wake events. ACPI defines the _SxW (where x could be 0,1,2, or 3, respective to each supported device state) objects to provide this information to the operating system. There is an SxW object for each supported system power state, Sx.

4. _CRS: _CRS is used to describe the resources for a device. Similar to _PRx, _CRS methods are defined in a particular device node scope and apply to that particular device.

5. _DSW: ACPI defines the _DSW object as a way for the operating system to inform the ACPI platform firmware about the next sleep or low-power idle period.

6. _PRW: _PRW is used to specify any additional power resource that may be needed for a device to be enabled for wake. _PRW is also used to define the wake capability for traditional PC platforms.

Similar to _PRx, _PRW methods are defined in a particular device node scope and apply to that particular device.

The ACPI code needs to provide these callbacks that are used by the ACPI framework. The code is based on the platform design. The mechanism enables a separation between the platform-specific operations and the platform-agnostic, device-specific operations. This allows the device drivers to focus on the platform-agnostic operations/flows and rely on the ACPI callbacks to do the platform-specific operations like switching on/off a particular power resource, and so on.

Real-Time Systems

A drone is a real-time system, meaning it has to process and respond to events within the stipulated maximum threshold time in order to avoid a system malfunction. Real-time systems run with resource and time constraints. In order to design a robust real-time system like a drone, we need to make specific design choices in HW and SW. The HW and SW considerations for a real-time system are discussed in the following sections.

Hardware

In a simple system, the control logic is easy to design. There could be one simple loop that checks for the events that need servicing and performs the necessary actions. However, as the system complexity grows (with multiple functions, events, and priorities), the control system complexity grows accordingly.

As control systems become more complicated, it is increasingly difficult to manage the various MCU functions with a simple control routine. With multiple events with different priorities, a single control loop just cannot get to every function quickly enough. And, for a real-time system, all events need be serviced within their required response time.

Timer

In order to satisfy the need, we need a real-time approach to control, which can ensure that events are serviced within their stipulated/required response times. One option for improving real-time response is to use a real-time operating system or RTOS. In this approach, every task in the control system can be assigned a time slice of the CPU processing cycle. If a particular function doesn't need the time allocated currently, it can "turn over" the time to another function so that precious processing cycles are not lost. Modern CPUs have been optimized to make it easy to implement RTOS implementations. One of the key features is inclusion of a dedicated timer that is used for determining processing allocation, which makes it easy to allocate time slices to functions/tasks.

Advanced Interrupt Controller

Because RTOS-based systems need to respond to real-time events quickly and efficiently, it is important to optimize the interrupt processing time. This is because, if the interrupt takes too many cycles to respond, real-time response will suffer. Also, if the device interrupts are multiplexed due to a lower number of interrupt lines/vector available on interrupt controller, the software will have to spend a lot of time trying to figure out the source of the interrupt (by reading all the devices that are multiplexed into a line). It is therefore necessary for the system to have an advanced interrupt controller to optimize the interrupt processing time.

Context Switching

While switching from one task/function to the other, there are a plenty of things that need to change: registers, memory, and so on. MCUs provide HW support for faster context switch and make it easier to have a predictable response time.

Memory

Ensuring required data and code availability to the MCU for operation is essential to meet the response time requirement. Even correctable faults (for example, page faults) can add unpredictable latency, which a real-time system may not be able to tolerate. In fact, the virtual memory system is one of the key contributors to the response time unpredictability.

Data Processing Throughput

The associated processing units/DSP should be capable of supporting the compute/processing requirement of the system.

Priority

Since in the real-time system top priority tasks should always run first (and should be able to preempt the current running process if a higher priority task comes in), there needs to be a mechanism to assign priorities to tasks, preempt the tasks based on priority, and context switch to the new task.

The SoC chosen for our reference drone design does support the above HW features and therefore is suitable for a real-time system design like a drone.

SW Considerations

In addition to the specific hardware considerations, there needs to be a few considerations during software design. It must be noted that the software considerations are for the same purpose or need: designing a real-time system that can respond and complete the work in a stipulated time, reliably.

Interrupt Handling

While discussing the HW consideration topic, optimized interrupt handling is essential to accomplish the real-time performance requirement. Because multiple interrupts are often present in the system, prioritization needs to happen. In other words, the most important task must always be serviced within predefined time constraints regardless of other events.

Also, the maximum contribution to the interrupt latency is due to non-reentrant or critical processing paths that must be completed before the interrupt can actually be processed.

Real-Time Operating Systems

There are so many operating systems available to choose from and most of the time there is no clear choice. We need to make tradeoffs in terms of capabilities and other features. At a high level, today there are two classes of operating systems used for real-time work: dedicated RTOSes designed exclusively for real-time applications and general-purpose operating systems that have been enhanced to provide real-time capability. The use of a real-time executive makes real-time performance feasible for a general-purpose operating system.

Real-Time Languages

In order to improve the real-time performance of the software system, the usage of specially designed real-time languages is helpful. Ada, HAL/S, and CHILL are a few real-time languages. Even though it is possible to use a general purpose language like C or Java, because of the special requirements of performance and reliability demanded by real-time systems, the choice of programming language is important. Many general purpose programming languages (e.g., C, FORTRAN, Modula-2), however, can be used effectively for real-time applications.

Task Synchronization and Communication

In a multi-tasking system there is a need for different tasks to pass information. There is also a need to have a synchronization mechanism across tasks. In a real-time system, semaphores are commonly used to implement and manage the mailboxes used for synchronization.

System Software Integration and Bring-Up

In the preceding sections, we talked about how to develop and/or procure the software components that are required for our drone software system design. Once these components are available, we need to integrate them to make the system. In the following sections, we will talk about the steps we have to follow to make a system out of these components.

System Bring-Up

The first step in making the system is to bring up the base system. Bringing up the core system means assembling the hardware, applying the firmware to boot the system, installing the operating system, and enabling the system interfaces. We need to follow a step-by-step procedure to bring up the system.

System Firmware

As you might imagine, the first step is to assemble the hardware as prescribed earlier. Once the hardware is assembled, the next step is to get the system firmware. The system firmware needs to be flashed in the SPI NOR (for our design choice). The system firmware is provided by the SoC vendor, and it may have multiple subcomponents depending on the SoC design/vendor. The SoC vendor provides the tools and mechanism for flashing the system firmware.

The system firmware is responsible for the system initialization. Please note that there are two components to the system firmware: the first is related to the SoC, and the other is related to the rest of the platform. The SoC-related part is responsible for initializing the SoC components and interfaces, and the platform-related component is responsible for initializing and setting up the rest of the components on the base board.

The platform-related component of the system firmware comes from the SoC vendor as a reference (based on the reference platform, the SoC vendor would have created it for internal consumption and validation). We need to make the changes based on platform design and components.

Once the system firmware is flashed and the system is powered up, the system will be able to boot to an built-in mini operating system (EFI shell). Since there is no other operating system installed yet, the BIOS boot up process will launch the EFI shell and stop there. The next step is to install RTLinux (the operating system we chose earlier).

OS (RTLinux)

As you know, RTLinux is basically a patch over the standard Linux kernel. RTLinux talks directly to the hardware and acts as a proxy for hardware to the Linux kernel. In order to install RTLinux, the first step is to compile the RTLinux patch for the specific Linux kernel version.

It should be noted that RTLinux versions and Linux kernel versions are two separate things. For our instance, we are going to use RTLinux 3.1. The kernel patch for Linux kernel 2.4.4 is named kernel_patch-2.4. Please note that the RTLinux kernel patch is available for other kernel versions as well: for example, kernel_patch-2.2.19 is for kernel 2.2.19.

The kernel and respective RTLinux patch need to be downloaded and patched. The Linux patching process is the same as applying any other patch to the kernel. After the patch process, the kernel and modules need to be built and installed. After the installation, we reboot the system and then configure and enable the RTLinux. Once Linux/RTLinux is installed, the system firmware boot up process will launch this new OS.

Drivers/Modules

In the RTLinux (Linux) world, the hardware drivers are developed as modules and compiled and installed. In the current context, drivers for a majority of the devices are already part of the mainstream kernel code. Please note that despite the fact that drivers may be part of the same source base, they may not be part of the kernel inherently. At the same time, once the modules are loaded, they become part of the kernel itself. The modules are loaded using the insmod command and removed from the kernel using the rmmod command. While developing modules, no libraries are linked to the modules/kernel and therefore we should not include any of the standard header files or use any of the functions from the standard libraries.

Figure 6-13 shows the Linux module's loading and unloading process. The insmod command calls the init function of the module and the rmmod calls the cleanup function of the module. The module developer is responsible for providing both functions.

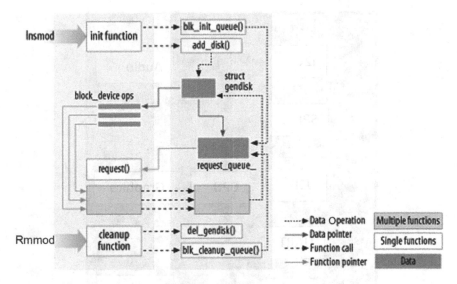

Figure 6-13. *Linux Module Loading Process*

In the typical scenario, the component vendors provide the driver/ module for customers. For our design as well, we procure the driver components from the respective vendors. Generally speaking, there are two types of components on our system.

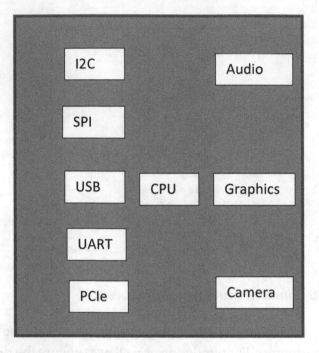

Figure 6-14. *Sample SoC block diagram*

1. There are controllers that are part of the SoC we chose. The internal block diagram of a sample SoC, for example, might look like Figure 6-14.

   As you can see, there are many controllers like I2C, SPI, USB, UART, PCIe, Audio, Graphics, and Camera/Imaging controllers on the SoC. In this case, the drivers for these controllers (within the SoC) are provided by the SoC vendor, unless they're already part of the OS by default.

2. The second category is those that are located on the
    board as discrete components and are connected
    to the controllers on the SoC. The cameras, sensors,
    and WiFi+BT modules fall into this category. These
    components are provided by separate vendors
    and the drivers are provided by the respective
    vendors, unless they're already part of the OS. When
    making the component/design choices, we need
    to investigate whether a driver (for the specific OS
    of choice) for the component is provided by the
    respective vendor. If the driver is not provided by the
    vendor, we need to develop a driver on our own by
    referring to the device/components specification.
    Given the fact that there are so many vendors and
    plenty of choices while choosing the components,
    there is almost no reason to choose a component
    that does not have a driver for the OS of our choice.
    There may be a remote case where we absolutely
    need to choose a component for which the driver is
    not available, and we must develop the driver on our
    own. However, it's best to avoid such a case since
    the time, effort, and resources required to develop a
    driver for a non-trivial component is significant.

Now that we have the drivers for the components on the system, we
must load the drivers for them to start operating. The drivers are written
as Linux loadable modules, and are loaded with the insmod command; to
remove or unload a driver, rmmod is used. Once these drivers are loaded
and start operating, we are ready for the application layer. The application
layer uses these drivers to interact with the hardware.

Libraries/Middle Layer and Application

As discussed, the application layer is responsible for bringing the system to life by means of supporting the intended usage. And libraries make the application development easier by means of providing commonly used functions, APIs, and framework. As far as the bring-up activity is concerned, libraries and applications are more or less the same. Both are user mode components. As discussed, the libraries we need (OpenCV and GStreamer) can be downloaded from the Web and installed, and we need to procure the application software (home grown or delivered by any one of the drone software providers), install it, and start using the same. There is also a need for remote control and monitoring software. This remote control and monitoring software runs remotely and connects to the drone system over the network/internet protocol. The application software can be developed and installed like any other standard application software.

Verification, Validation, and Maintenance

Once we have all the software components put together, we need to ensure that the components individually and as a whole system meet the requirements. There are various aspects of requirements, such as functional, performance, stability, reliability, and security. Verification and validation ensure that the systems meet all of these different requirements.

Verification and validation are related but slightly different practices. Verification is the process of evaluating software to determine whether the product at a given development phase satisfies the conditions imposed at the start of that phase. Verification is static practice of verifying documents, design, and code. Review, inspection, and "walk through" are some of the mechanisms to carry out verification. Another key point to note is that verification can determine whether the software is of high quality or not; however, it doesn't ensure that the system is functionally good.

Validation, on the other hand, is the process of evaluating the product at the end of development to determine whether it satisfies specified requirements. It is a dynamic process and is accomplished by various kinds of testing and end user trials. There are various types of testing, categorized based on different parameters: mechanism, methodology, and level. In the following sections, we will do quick survey of the various types and methodologies, and make a decision on what kind of testing and methodologies apply to our system.

Based on the Mechanism

Based on the mechanism applied for testing, the testing can be categorized as follows:

- *Manual testing*: It is carried out manually. Manual testing requires a lot of people and resources, and therefore limits the coverage.

- *Automated testing*: Automated testing uses software and tools to test a system. Some of the software and tools are developed to carry out a specific type of testing; therefore, we may need to use many different tools to cover all of the aspects of testing.

Based on the Methodology

Based on the methodology applied to the testing, the testing can be categorized as follows:

- *Black box testing*: In black box testing, tests are defined, designed, and performed without knowing and/or worrying about the internal implementation. It only relies on the inputs provided and expected output.

- *White box testing*: In white box testing, the internal implementation is known to the tester and the test cases and inputs are chosen by the tester, keeping in mind the internal implementation.

- *Gray box testing*: As the name indicates, gray box testing is a combination of black and white box testing. In this case, the tester has some knowledge of the implementation (at least the high-level interactions), but doesn't know all the low-level implementation detail, and the test case definition follows accordingly.

Based on the Testing Level

- *Functional testing*: As part of the functional testing, the system is tested against the functional requirement. There are different levels of functional testing:

  - *Unit testing*: During unit testing, individual units of source code like functions and classes are tested in isolation.

  - *Integration testing*: During the integration testing, multiple modules are put together and tested as a group.

  - *Smoke and sanity testing*: As part of the smoke testing, right after the build/integration, some sets of tests are performed to ascertain that critical functionalities of the software system are working fine. Sanity tests are performed, focusing on the specific fixes/changes in mind. The intent is to ascertain whether the fix looks reasonable to go ahead with further testing.

- *System testing*: In system testing, the testing happens at the system level (with respect to expected system functionality) to ensure that the system meets the specified system requirements.

- *Regression testing*: The regression testing ensures that the changes to the software don't break the existing functionalities (in a way that adversely affects the system).

- *User acceptance testing (UAT)*: UAT is performed to ensure that the system meets the stated end use requirements. There are two stages in UAT: the alpha testing is done on the developer side, while the beta testing is done on the end user/consumer side. UAT is also known as end user testing (EUT) or acceptance testing (AT).

- *End-to-end testing*: End-to-end testing is performed to exercise the complete flow of the application/ software system. It is usually done after system testing, and is carried out in a real-world scenario and environment.

- *Non-functional testing*: There are many nonfunctional tests carried out to ensure various aspects of the system. Some of the key non-functional test categories are summarized below:

  - *Performance testing*: Performance testing is carried out to ensure that the performance needs of the software/system are met in terms of speed, scalability, stability, and reliability.

- *Load testing*: Load testing is performed to check the system behavior under both normal and anticipated peak load conditions.

- *Stress testing*: Stress testing is performed to check the system behavior at load beyond the anticipated peak load conditions (and what the system can handle). This is done by driving an unusually high load on the system.

- *Security testing*: Security testing is performed to ensure that the system is safe from attacks like SQL injection, DoS, identity spoofing, cross-site scripting (XSS), and more. There are tools to statically analyze the software and identify potential security issues.

Now coming back to our drone system software, we apply both manual and automated testing. We apply different coverage to different components/areas: for the components availed from third parties (external world), we apply black box testing, while for internally developed components we apply gray box testing mixed with white box testing. As far as the functional test is concerned, all of the stages are performed for the software components developed internally, while for the components procured from external sources (third parties) we start with integration testing and go all the way to end-to-end testing. Security testing is part and parcel, and one of the most important aspects of overall validation.

Maintenance is about ensuring that the critical needs of software are met in terms of bug fixes and critical feature upgrades to keep the system running. In our case, we do not plan to upgrade the drone software with new features; however, we will need to fix any critical bugs if and when identified.

Conclusion

In this chapter, we discussed the drone software design and development. We discussed the software development life cycle, the software stack, and drone software design considerations, followed by the system bring-up, validation, and maintenance. The specifics of the components and features will depend on the purpose and design of the drone. However, the overall flow and process will remain similar for any drone software design.

CHAPTER 7

Drone Product Certification

Product certification or product qualification is the process of certifying that am electronic product has passed performance tests and quality assurance tests and meets qualification criteria stipulated in contracts, regulations, and specifications.

Right from the outset, products must comply with certain regulations that determine what substances and materials they can be made of and in what concentrations, and even where and how the products can be manufactured.

These regulations are in place to protect the public and the environment from toxic substances, to work towards the elimination of human rights violations in factories and mines, and to reduce violence in third-world countries. The general public may not realize just how hard companies work to make sure their products are safe and maintain an ethical supply chain, nor do some professionals fully grasp how comprehensive these regulations actually are.

The crop squad drone is no exception. The drone has to pass the general electronic device regulations and additional drone-specific regulations and certifications.

In fact, there are so many regulations that companies hire entire teams to work behind the scenes to make sure the final products are compliant.

© Neeraj Kumar Singh, Porselvan Muthukrishnan, Satyanarayana Sanpini 2019
N. K. Singh et al., *Industrial System Engineering for Drones*,
https://doi.org/10.1007/978-1-4842-3534-8_7

Each country has its own accreditation bodies/standards organizations and certification marking. The certification specification, test methods, and frequency of testing are published by the standards organization.

There are many third-party certification centers or labs, which are usually accredited by the product certification bodies. Product manufacturers can choose any of these centers to get certification for their products.

Regulatory Certification

The electronics industry has experienced a continuous pressure in product regulatory compliance mainly caused by the increase in the number of regulations that product designers and manufacturers need to abide by in order to put products into the marketplace.

These certifications qualify the products and their characteristics and are aimed at reducing the impact to health, minimizing security threats, and being respectful to the environment. The European Union has nearly 500 active laws in 2016 (such as RoHS, REACH, and WEEE) and tops the list of market regions with the most regulations issued per annum. The US follows with almost 200 (the FDA among others), and Asia and Central and South America have nearly 150 active laws each in 2016. In recent years, countries in Central and South America and Asia have become more concerned with the environmental impact of electronic products; thus they also have drafted and passed more environmental bills.

All types of electronic devices, including drones, must comply the following list of standards to get the marking or certification.

Safety

The board, accessories, and the system (including power supply, chassis, and all contents) should comply and to be tested to all the applicable safety standards, such as IEC for safety. Testing must be performed at accredited labs. Passing test reports must be provided to a product regulatory engineer for review and approval.

A drone is an electromechanical device, and all of the below mentioned tests are mandatory before launching one into the market.

Electrical

Electrical safety testing is essential to ensure safe operating standards for any product that uses electricity.

To get the approval from different certifying agencies for respective countries, the product must pass safety tests such as the high voltage test, insulation resistance test, ground bond and ground continuity test, and leakage current test. More details of these tests are described in IEC 60335, IEC 61010, and many other national and international standards documents.

Drones run on electricity so it's very important for a drone to pass the electrical safety test.

Functional

Functional safety is essential to ensure the system is free of risk of physical injury or of damage to the health of people either directly or indirectly.

Unlike automotive, aerospace, and medical systems, there is no stringent functional safety standard for drones as of today. As the market for commercial drones matures, more stringent certification requirements are expected to be established.

Drones are more common for commercial and industrial applications. The increase in drone usage is raising safety concerns and this will make the standards more stringent in future.

More details are available in IEC 61508, which is the generic functional standard for electrical and electronic systems.

Mechanical

It is essential to check the fast-moving blades or propellers as well as the conditions under which a mechanical failure of the drones could pose a potential safety risk to users. Also, drones are checked to make sure there are no sharp edges to cause injuries while handling or non-operation of drone systems.

All of the external parts of a drone are continuously moving. Some drones may have sharp blades used as propellers, so mechanical safety is very important.

Chemical

Chemical safety certification is to make sure users are not exposed to life-threatening chemicals used in the system. Chemicals are found everywhere; whether they are naturally present in raw materials or added to create specific characteristics, they have become a heavily regulated area. All the chemicals should be assessed and tested to protect users from unnecessary risks.

Different parts of the drone use different materials: metal, plastic, or fiber, based on the requirements. The chemicals used for the mechanical parts and hardware are assessed carefully to make sure they are safe for the environment.

Battery

Millions of products, from laptops to cell phones to watches and more recently electric/hybrid vehicles and drones, contain batteries.

With the increase in applications for these batteries, it has become apparent that there are some safety issues that need to be addressed. Batteries can catch fire if they are damaged, exposed to high temperatures (exceeding 290°F), or packaged incorrectly. Lithium-ion battery thermal runaway reactions can exceed 1,220 °F, the melting point of aluminum, a key material in airplane construction. Lithium-metal battery fires are far hotter yet.

For example, a UPS cargo plane that was carrying thousands of lithium batteries crashed near Dubai in the United Arab Emirates, killing both pilots. The accident is still under investigation, but preliminary reports indicate that investigators have focused much of their attention on the batteries, which may have started a fire onboard the plane.

As a result, the organizations that now govern the transportation of lithium and lithium-ion batteries and cells include the International Civil Aviation Organization (ICAO), the International Air Transport Association (IATA), and the International Maritime Dangerous Goods Code (IMDG). In addition to international requirements, domestic regulations must be followed. The United States Department of Transportation (DOT) regulates the shipment of lithium and lithium-ion cells and batteries domestically under part 49 of the Code of Federal Regulations and UN/DOT under Section 38.3.

To properly address the safety issue and decrease the failure rate, new standards have been instituted. The required compliance to the new IEC 62133 standard means testing needs to be completed before the battery products can be shipped and domestic shipments must be tested in accordance with UN 38.3.

This standard specifies requirements and tests for the safe operation of portable, sealed secondary cells and batteries. Cells and batteries need to be designed and constructed so that they are safe under conditions of both intended use and reasonably foreseeable misuse.

Emission

Emission testing is the part of Electromagnetic Compatibly (EMC) regulation on any electronic devices including drones. The goal of emission testing is to protect the radio spectrum to enable radio services to operate and to ensure that electrical interference is minimized.

Most EMC standards throughout the world are based on a CISPR standard (the International Special Committee on Radio Interference). As indicated in the name, CISPR is a special committee of the IEC (International Electrotechnical Commission) whose remit is to prepare and issue standards for various product types such that radio services are protected.

All EMC standards find their origins in CISPR standards irrespective of their actual name. FCC Parts 15 and 18 (USA), for example, are derived from CISPR 16, 11, and 22.

Radiated

Radiation testing involves measuring the electromagnetic field strength of the emissions that are unintentionally generated by the electronic product or drones. Emissions are inherent to the switching voltages and currents within any digital circuit. The intent of radiation testing is to ensure that radiation levels are within specified acceptable levels.

Conducted

Conducted emissions are internal electromagnetic emissions propagated along a power or signal conductor, creating noise. The noise is subsequently transferred to the equipment. This test method is used to measure conducted emissions on power leads and antenna terminals.

Immunity

Immunity testing is just the application of some electromagnetic phenomena to the drone product. It is the opposite of emissions testing. Instead of measuring what's coming from your product, immunity testing involves subjecting your product to radio waves.

Radiated

Radiated field susceptibility testing typically involves a high-powered source of RF or EM pulse energy and a radiating antenna to direct the energy at the potential victim or device under test (the drone). This checks the capability and operation of the drone even in the presence of an external interference signal propagated via free space.

Conducted

This method is used to determine whether equipment is susceptible to external electromagnetic energy injected on its power leads, antenna ports, and interconnecting cables. Conducted voltage and current susceptibility testing typically involve a high-powered signal or pulse generator and a current clamp or other type of transformer to inject the test signal. The conducted susceptibility is performed to determine a drone's ability to operate in the presence of an external interference signal propagated via a conductor. This usually happens in the power supply mains or from the battery terminals.

Transient immunity is also tested against powerline disturbances including surges, lightning strikes, and switching noise. In motor vehicles or drones, the tests are also performed on battery terminals. It is implicit that the immunity should be as per the standard allowed limits.

Electrostatic Discharge

Electrostatic discharge (ESD) is the sudden flow of electricity between two electrically charged objects caused by contact, an electrical short, or dielectric breakdown. A buildup of static electricity can be caused by turbocharging or by electrostatic induction. Electronic devices need to be tested for ESD to prevent the device from damage during operation, static, or packaging transportation.

Electrostatic discharge testing is typically performed with a piezo spark generator called an "ESD pistol." Higher energy pulses, such as lightning or nuclear EMP simulations, can require a large current clamp or a large antenna that completely surrounds the drone. Some antennas are so large that they are located outdoors, and care must be taken not to cause an EMP hazard to the surrounding environment.

Electrical Fast Transient

The EFT immunity test is an attempt to simulate switching of inductive loads in the real world. A few examples of inductive load switching that could perceivably affect your product are bundled cables can capacitive couple disturbances from switched loads other cables, motors, and relays and toggling the switch nearby. These immunity tests are conducted while charging the drone through an AC adapter. This test proves that drone's functionality is not affected by any fast changing voltages in the power supply input.

Environmental Certification

Environmental testing certification is done for all the electronic devices to make sure they meet certain operating conditions as per the regulatory standards. This is applicable for drones.

Most certification services have a logo that can be applied to products certified under their standards. This is seen as a form of corporate social responsibility, allowing companies to address their obligation to minimize the harmful impacts to the environment by voluntarily following a set of externally set and measured objectives.

Product designers have to choose to comply with specific standards and validate against them with the help of certification companies. All the components chosen for the product must comply with these standards and criteria.

Temperature

Each component manufacturer defines its own operating temperature grades so designers must pay close attention to actual datasheet specifications. Most common temperature grades are

- Commercial: 0 °C to 70 °C

- Industrial: −40 °C to 85 °C

- Military: −55 °C to 125 °C

The environmental testing and validation is done in two stages. First, the boards without enclosures are kept inside the thermal chamber in operating condition. The chamber temperature is varied between -40, 25 (Ambient) and 85 °C as per the temperature change profile specified in the standards. Usually the temperature change rate should not exceed 2 °C. The same procedure is repeated for the boards inside the enclosures, which are drones. This certifies the drones, if it operates in that specified temperature range without any issues as specified by the standard.

The drone system should also meet the storage temperature range. The drone system is kept inside the chamber, non-operational. The drone is stored for days in an extended temperature, usually -40 to 125 °C for industrial. After few days, the device is powered on in the ambient temperature. If the device is functional without any failures, it complies with the industrial storage temperature regulations.

Humidity

Prolonged exposure to humidity can cause serious damage to electronic products. Drones must pass the humidity requirement, which can be tested in the humidity chamber. Humidity testing is combined with temperature and altitude testing in most cases, to match real-world conditions. The drone must be operable between 10%-90% relative humidity, a most common standard requirement for any electronic product.

Altitude

High altitude simulation testing provides insight into the integrity and durability of products that are frequently operated, installed, stored, or transported in elevated conditions. Similar to humidity, altitude is usually combined with pressure. The system is validated and certified in different altitude and pressure conditions.

The commercial drones are allowed to fly as long as they stay in the visual range of the user. There are strict rules for flying drones in different countries. All the drones used for commercial and industrial are low-altitude drones. Drones flying above 400 meters from sea level have to obtain special permission from the regulating bodies.

Apart from operational altitude, the storage altitude needs to be tested. This validates the drones for packaging and shipment in higher altitudes.

Drop, Shock, and Vibration

Mechanical testing includes drop, shock, and vibration testing. The most common tests are 6-axis vibration (sine or random), drop shock (half-sine or random), and drop test on the floor (with or without the package). This qualifies the drone for certain standards and ensures the durability, robustness, and performance of the drones.

Generally, the requirement criteria are as follows:

- *Packaged shock (drop)*: 6 face drops, 2 corner drops, and 3 edge drops for a total of 11 drops from a height of 36 inches if package weight < 20 pounds (30 inches if package weight ≥ 20 to < 40 pounds).

- *Packaged vibration*: 0.015 g2/Hz from 5 Hz to 40 Hz, sloping to 0.00015 g2/Hz at 500 Hz (slope down), input acceleration is 1.09 gRMS, 1 hour per axis for all 3 axes for all samples; random control limit tolerance is ± 3 dB.

Reliability

As per a new study, electronics failures are the cause of 25% of all failures, the rest being attributed to weather and pilot error. Drone systems provide increasing protection against human-induced failures and enhanced performance through improvements in flight control software. These systems also have multiple sensors to detect and predict deterioration or failures. However, the low-cost commercial systems attractive to some of the leaner and cost-sensitive small-to-midsized businesses may not have the same level of redundancy to provide failsafe operations. This places a greater reliance on the reliability of each electronic component as control software improves and the balance of high-end redundant systems vs. less redundant low-to mid-range systems shifts. This is in no small part due to the relative complexity of the electronics in drone systems.

Service and Support

The ODM should include a manual and authorized service center partner listed for support. This will help the user to inspect the aircraft completely and to determine any issue and also the procedure to fix it. The user should able to solve any small fixes or should be able to estimate the repair cost and needed parts with the help of an authorized technical team. The local service centers should be able to fix any kinds of issues of the drone.

Pilot Distribution

Pilot testing provides an opportunity to identify the system-level bugs before the product launch. It also helps to fine-tune the final system.

A limited number of users are identified from the designers, test engineers, and customers for the pilot distribution. Inputs are taken from the users for fine tuning the system. Authorized service centers receive the pilot product for the required training for service and repair.

Device Software Upgrade

The final drone product provides a simple mechanism accessible to the user or the service personnel for device software upgrades through a laptop, PC, or directly from a wireless network.

Technical Service

The final product is accompanied by a technical user manual to enable the user or the service personal to easily configure the device. The user manual should include the brand new drone assembly fresh from the box (assembling the discrete parts like propellers and landing gears if shipped as separate components) and how to replace the broken drone parts. The accompanying technical service manual can be either a hard copy or an electronic copy or a website link.

Product Ecology

Products get qualified and approved by a product ecology engineer or scientist. An ecology engineer closely works with the designers to make sure the components, processing, and manufacturing are compliant with global environmental standards.

The component, PCB, and product manufacturers provide the test reports and corresponding collaterals for the ecological engineers for review up on request.

Prohibited Substances

Any component in the electrical BOM, system BOM, or the processes such as manufacturing and assembly should not contain any of the below listed prohibited substances. Most of the vendor datasheets and device collaterals specify the restrictions of hazardous substances and compliance. If not mentioned, the document must be available upon the request from the vendor.

ID substance/Reportable applications/Reporting threshold:

- Asbestos/All/Intentionally added

- Fluorinated greenhouse gases (PFC, SF6, HFC)/All/ Intentionally added

- Mercury/Mercury compounds/All, except batteries/ Intentionally added or 0.1 mass% of total Hg in homogenous material

- Ozone-depleting substances (CFC, Halon, HBFC, HCFC, and others)/All/Intentionally added

- Perfluorooctane sulfonates (PFOS)/All/Intentionally added or 0.1 mass% in material

- Phenol, 2-(2Hbenzotriazol-2-yl)-4,6-bis (1,1-dimethlethyl) CAS number 3846-71-7/All/ Intentionally added

- Polybrominated biphenyls (PBBs)/All/0.1 mass% in homogenous material

- Polybrominated diphenylethers (PBDEs)/All/0.1 mass% in homogenous material

- Polychlorinated biphenyls (PCBs) and specific substitutes/All/Intentionally added

- Polychlorinated terphenyls (PCTs)/All/0.005 mass% in material

- Polychlorinated naphthalenes (PCNs)/All/Intentionally added

- Radioactive substances/All/Intentionally added

- Shortchain Chlorinated Paraffins (C10 – C13)/All/0.1 mass%

- Tributyl Tin Oxide (TBTO) CAS Number 56-35-9/All/ Intentionally added or 0.1 mass%

ROHS

RoHS (Restriction of Hazardous Substances Directive) is the directive that restricts the use of ten hazardous materials in the manufacturing of various types of electronic and electrical equipment. Initially there were six; four were added during 2015. The designers have to make sure the product is free of these hazardous materials.

RoHS restricts the use of the following ten substances:

- Lead (Pb)

- Mercury (Hg)

- Cadmium (Cd)

- Hexavalent chromium (Cr6+)

- Polybrominated biphenyls (PBB)

- Polybrominated diphenyl ether (PBDE)

- Bis(2-ethylhexyl) phthalate (DEHP)

- Butyl benzyl phthalate (BBP)

- Dibutyl phthalate (DBP)

- Diisobutyl phthalate (DIBP)

EU REACH

The product manufacturer needs to establish and maintain a robust business process for tracking new EU Registration, Evaluation and Authorization of Chemical (REACH) candidate list substances of very high concern (SVHCs) as they are posted on the ECHA website and to identify new reporting obligations.

Devices must be compliant with REACH Regulation EU NO 1907/2006 and latest REACH SVHC list. EU REACH SVHCs above the reporting threshold in articles supplied to the actual product owners or designers upon listing of the SHVC on the candidate lists along with Safe Use directions and location of substances in the device(s).

The manufacturer must also provide test reports for the standards such as IEC 62474, IPC 1752 Class 5/6, or negative declarations demonstrating compliance of cables, power cords, and power adaptors.

Negative REACH declarations are acceptable if approved or waived by the product ecology engineer.

California Proposition 65

California Proposition 65 protects the public from toxic substances that may cause cancer and birth defects and reduces or eliminates exposures to those chemicals generally, for example in consumer products, by requiring warnings in advance of exposure.

If the device contains cables, power cords, or power adaptors, all shall meet the California Proposition 65 requirements. The manufacturers must provide documentation and/or test reports that show compliance. In the event that California Proposition 65 substances are over the reporting threshold or intentionally added, the device must be labeled with the appropriate warning label. If the substance threshold is over the reportable level, the manufacturer must specify the chemical, location, and concentration.

WEEE

The WEEE directive sets collection, recycling, and recovery targets for all types of electrical goods, with a minimum rate of 4 kilograms per head of population per annum recovered for recycling by 2009. The RoHS directive sets restrictions upon European manufacturers as to the material content of new electronic equipment placed on the market.

All devices must comply with the WEEE (Waste Electrical and Electronic Equipment) directive EN 50419. The WEEE marking must be on the board or system.

ISO

All manufacturers must be ISO-9001 certified and must have in place a Hazardous Substance Program Management program.

Product Certification Centers

Since the certification equipment is fairly costly and it is a very specialized skill to make drones, manufactures use the services of product certification centers. Product certification centers offer a full range of testing and certification services including pre-assessment, gap analysis, batch testing, and full compliance testing. The certification centers specialize in the job and cater services to various different manufactures.

Device Costing

Costing is very important when bringing a new physical product to market. It's even more challenging for those bringing a complex product such as a drone to market. BOM costing starts during the architecture phase itself.

Apart from the BOM cost, other costs such manufacturing and life cycle costs add to the final product cost.

Costing varies throughout the product design cycle. The product cost is different for proof of concept, prototype/pilot, and the actual product.

Production Cost

The production cost influences the final product cost. The final individual product cost is the outcome of total mass volume product cost and non-recurring engineering and manufacturing cost.

Production costs are the direct materials, direct labor, and manufacturing overhead used to manufacture products. The production costs are also referred to as manufacturing costs, product costs, a manufacturer's inventorial costs, or the costs occurring in the factory.

Accessories Cost

Many products offer optional accessories bought separately for the product by the user. Some drones are designed in such a way that they can be used with third-party accessories or components.

Drone Regulations

Before flying the drone, the user need to be aware of the rules and regulations that the Federal Aviation Administration (FAA) has put in place for flying drones in the US. There are similar regulations in other countries. The user also should be aware of the regulations and the rights of those around the flying drone.

The drone product has to include the rules or a document so that the user has easy access to regulations in order to educate him/herself.

Regulations

The basic rules for flying a drone are the following: fly the drone below 400 feet from the ground level; keep the drone within sight; never fly in the no-fly zone specified by the government; never fly over a crowded area; never fly under the influence; and never fly during an emergency situation like a fire.

Drone Registration

It is mandatory to register the drone and the pilot, if used for commercial and outdoor. However, non-commercial, indoor usage does not require any registration for the drone or the pilot.

Toy drones, which are tiny and weigh less than 8.8 ounces (250g), do not require registration. All other drones need to be registered for outdoor usage.

Summary

Acquiring the necessary certifications closes the industrial drone design process, and the drone product is officially ready to be shipped to the retail stores or the customers directly.

Once the drone product is out in the market, the marketing team starts their research again on the new market trends or new feature addition. All the limitations and technology gaps will be filled usually in the next revision products. This product life cycle goes on and on, not only for drones, but for any kind of electronic product.

APPENDIX I

Schematics Basics

Schematics are the primary document to design, build and troubleshoot the hardware.

Mostly, the architecture or functional blocks are split in to schematics pages and connected together. There might be separate sections for each subsystems, power delivery and Interconnects. Every electrical subsystem is covered in the schematics. The pages are sequenced in such a way the designer or the test engineers later navigate easily block by block. There are BKMs available for schematics to make it more presentable aesthetically, readable and easily understandable later during the design review and testing phase.

The components or symbols within the page or across the pages are connected through wires called nets. The point to point nets are connected with unique signal names. Signal names are based on the electrical interface type. There are global nets like power nodes, which might be connecting many devices run throughout the schematics pages.

Different components use different reference designators to identify in schematics.

Understanding how to read and follow schematics is an important skill for any electronics engineer.

© Neeraj Kumar Singh, Porselvan Muthukrishnan, Satyanarayana Sanpini 2019
N. K. Singh et al., *Industrial System Engineering for Drones*,
https://doi.org/10.1007/978-1-4842-3534-8

Some of the standard basic schematics symbols of various components are given below

Resistor

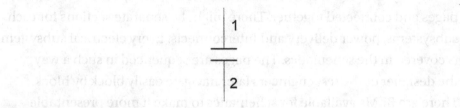

Capacitor

Inductor

Diode

Three Pin Header/Connector

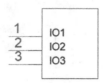

IC (20 Pin Buffer)

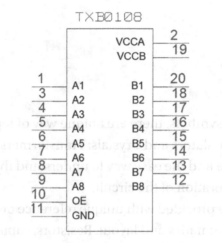

TACT Switch with mounting holes (M1..M4)

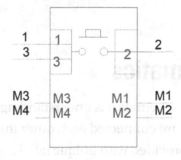

Power Source

Ground

Transistor

Similar to these symbols, there are unique way of representing Logic Gates, Op AMPs, Oscillators and Crystals, Transformers, Fuses, Relays etc. Schematics is simple and the easy way to understand the components, connections and operation of the circuit.

Each part will be provided with unique reference designators to identify from the schematics and layout. Resistors, capacitors, inductors and other discrete are identified with values and other details. While integrated circuits are identified with part numbers along with the version numbers.

Reading Schematics

First step in reading the schematics is understanding the components. And how those components are connected each other through nets and nodes. Each net name will be provided with unique labels.

Below is the Board to Board connector with net connections provided with unique NetNames.

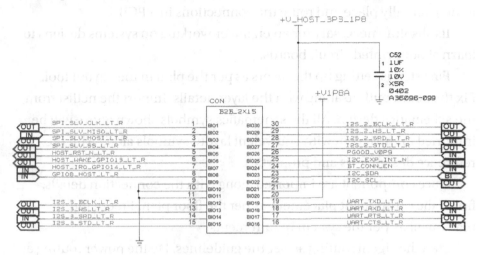

Usually schematics should be split into different functional blocks and distributed through multiple pages. Most schematics drawn sequentially from the power input towards system boot flow. There is not standard practice to draw a schematics. The best practice to present is to keep the inputs at the left side and outputs at the right side of each block for easy understanding.

Layout Basics

PCB layout design has been around for decades, but its relevance not faded yet. There are lot of customization and miniaturization done over the time to get smaller PCBs for wearable devices. In the age of where everyday devices with embedded systems are becoming Internet-connected devices, PCB design is still meeting that need, while growing more advanced, and more in demand.

237

Despite so much advancements in the PCB technology and the design tools, the layout CAD design still same. Skilled CAD design engineers have to do manually place and route the connections in a PCB.

Its absolute necessary for an engineer working on systems designs to learn about printed circuit boards.

First step is setting up the layers as per the plan in the Layout tool. Fix the board outline along with the layer details. Import the netlist from the schematics design. All the schematics symbols shown above will be imported in the layout with equivalent layout symbols along with the reference designators and properties.

Once component are imported along with the connection details, finish the component placement as per the floor plan. Freeze the placement as per the system requirements.

Start the signal routing as per the guidelines. Do the power routing at the end.

Designers can view the board file on the Layout viewer, navigate layer by layer and make sure everything done as per electrical guidelines. Do not violate laws of physics anywhere in the design.

Electronic System Design Communication interfaces

Interfacing the electronic system allows the electronic circuit or system to communicate internally and externally. The communications interface allows the transmission of either analogue signals or digital data.

Each electronic system communicates with other systems by transmitting data via a transmitter (Tx) subsystem and receives data via a receiver (Rx) subsystem. The medium between the two systems is the communications channel. However, when analogue signals or digital data are transmitted through the communications channel, noise might be added to the signal, potentially corrupting the data. A great deal of care must be taken to ensure that the electronic systems do not use corrupted information.

Although information can be sent or received as analogue signals or digital data, digital data transmission is increasingly common and occurs as either parallel or serial data transmission:

Parallel data transmission. Multiple bits of data are transferred simultaneously, allowing high-speed data transfer.

Serial data transmission. One bit of data is transferred at a time (a serial bitstream). Serial data transmission takes longer, but when the data is transmitted on electrical wires (typically copper wires), fewer wires are required than with the parallel data transmission. Serial data transmission also lends itself to data transmission via optical fibers and wireless methods.

Many systems allow several parallel and serial communications standards

For the synchronous data transfer, a separate clock is shown for the transmitter and receiver. In practice, there might only be one common clock for the transmitter and receiver.

During data transmission, errors can occur when noise is added to the signal and when the noise is large enough to corrupt the data being transmitted. The transmitter circuit can include the ability to add information to the data before they are transmitted, and the receiver circuit can include the ability to identify whether the data it has received appears to be OK or has been corrupted. A simple method for error checking is to use parity checking, in which a bit is added and transmitted with the data. Considering a byte of data (8 bits) as an example, parity checking is of two types:

Odd parity coding will set the parity bit to a logic 1 if the number of logic 1s in the byte is even, so that the total number of logic 1s is an odd number. If the receiver receives an odd number of logic 1s, then it will identify that the byte was transmitted correctly.

Even parity coding will set the parity bit to a logic 1 if the number of logic 1s in the byte is odd, so that the total number of logic 1s is an even number. If the receiver receives an even number of logic 1s, then it will identify that the byte was transmitted correctly.

Parity checking is a rudimentary method, and most communications systems include more sophisticated capabilities.

The characteristics of the channel must also be considered, the data may need to be modulated before transmission. Modulation takes either of two forms:

Baseband signals in digital are the 1s and 0s being generated. On a PCB and communicating between ICs on the PCB, baseband signals are used. These signals cover a frequency range from DC to an upper frequency value.

Modulated signals are baseband signals that have been modulated by a carrier signal so that the entire signal is now at some higher frequency. Modulation allows the baseband signals to be transmitted through a particular communications channel. When modulated signals are transmitted and received, the electronic system must include a modulator and a demodulator.

The transmission of the signal through the communications channel can be either one-way or two-way, so the designer must decide whether the communication is to be simplex, half-duplex, or full-duplex:

Simplex, in which data transmission is one-way on a single channel.

Half-duplex, in which data transmission is two-way on a single channel. This means that the direction of data transmission alternates, so that the system would be able to receive or transmit, but not both at the same time.

Full-duplex, in which data transmission is two-way on two channels. This means that an electronic system would be able to receive or transmit at the same time.

Finally, the signal will be transmitted through the communications channel via electrical wires, optical fibers, or using wireless methods.

Wired, in which metal wires, typically copper, are used to transmit the electrical signal.

Optical fiber, in which an electrical signal is converted to an optical (light) signal and transmitted along the optical fiber. This allows high transmission rates and low loss, so that signals can be transmitted over long distances, and a low bit error rate. The electrical signal is generated either by a light-emitting diode (LED) creating noncoherent light or by a laser creating coherent light. At the receiver end, the signal is converted back to an electrical signal using a photodiode or phototransistor.

Wireless, in which an electrical signal is modulated and applied to an antenna. The more popular modulation methods are AM (amplitude modulation), FM (frequency modulation), and PM (phase modulation). The signal is transmitted through free space, and at the receiver, another antenna picks up the transmitted signal, demodulates it, and restores it. It must then be amplified before it can be used.

High Speed Interfaces

High-speed serial interfaces are successful in chips due to demand for high bandwidth and performance of electronic devices. Various standards are developed around different high speed interfaces in a single monolithic IC. However, different standards also have different requirements and from a silicon design perspective. Creating a high speed interface cell that meets the requirements of different standards becomes a smart design proposition.

Only by understanding the differences among emerging high-speed interface standards and the tradeoffs involved in a common implementation will the system designer will better be able to choose the right device for his application.

Basically, a given high speed link can be modeled with three elements: the transmitter, a channel that propagates the signal, and a receiver:

The channel may be as simple as a pc board trace used to interconnect two chips or it may be much more complicated - for example, for a WAN backplane application the "channel" may have multiple lengths of pc board trace joined by connectors. For long-reach standards the channel may also have optics since long reach is required.

In an ideal system, the edges of a digital signal will always occur at integer multiples of the signal period. In a real system, the edges of a digital signal will occur in a distribution around the center point, which is the average period of the digital signal.

Jitter is defined as the variation in the edge placement of a digital signal. Three jitter components are usually specified: jitter generation, jitter tolerance, and jitter transfer. Jitter generation is the amount of jitter created by a device assuming the device's reference clock to be jitter-free. Jitter tolerance is the maximum amount of jitter a device can withstand and still reliably receive data. Jitter transfer is a measure of the amount of jitter transferred from the receive side of a device to the transmit side of a device.

Jitter requirements for high-speed interface standards vary widely. Deterministic jitter is jitter generated by either insufficient channel bandwidth, leading to inter-symbol-interference, or by duty-cycle distortion, which leads to timing errors in data clocking. Random jitter is usually assumed to have a Gaussian distribution and is generated by physical noise such as thermal noise. Sinusoidal jitter is used to test the jitter tolerance of a receiver across a range of jitter frequencies and is not a jitter type that would be encountered in a deployed system.

Multiple approaches to meet the jitter requirements can be taken. Since many of these high-bandwidth interfaces use source-synchronous clocks, the jitter in the generated clock is of concern. Such systems benefit from using a high-quality crystal and PLL to generate the board clock used to clock most of the system logic, since clocks recovered from the received data usually have high jitter relative to a quality crystal oscillator.

Pre-emphasis may be applied to the output signals to ensure the received signal has a well-defined shape after the frequency-dependent deleterious effects of the channel are taken into consideration. PLLs required by the clock-and-data-recovery circuits in the receivers must be able to accurately track the input data. The receivers may also use equalization to reshape the received pulse and "open the eye" of the received signal.

Pulse-shaping

The pre-emphasis and equalization techniques described above are methods of pulse-shaping where the shape of the waveform is modified to "open-up" the eye diagram. Pre-emphasis is done by emphasizing the high frequency content of the output waveform and is done by the transmitter. Equalization is done by emphasizing the high frequency content of the input waveform and is done by the receiver. The emphasis on the high-frequency content is required since the channel frequency response is a low-pass response.

One simpler common pre-emphasis technique is to temporarily increase the rail voltage of the transmitter for 0-1 or 1-0 transitions. With this technique the rise and fall times for the circuit are accelerated, since after the transition the output is allowed to "settle" to a voltage closer to the common-mode voltage for a continuous run of common symbols. This technique has the advantage of requiring minimal circuit area to implement, since it can be done using digital logic — complex analog filters are not required.

An example differential interface architecture used by many CMOS differential circuits, The transmitter may be AC- or DC-coupled to the receiver. For DC-coupling, the transmitter output lines are directly connected to the receiver input lines - so any DC voltage on the transmitter output line is presented to the receiver input line. The common-mode voltage of a DC-coupled receiver will therefore vary as the common-mode voltage of the transmitter varies.

For an AC-coupled link, the transmitter output lines are connected to the receiver input lines through series capacitors, which serve as DC-blockers. An AC-coupled receiver can control its common-mode voltage, since the AC-coupling capacitor serves as a DC block - the transmitter cannot vary the common-mode voltage of the receiver. AC-coupling is possible because the maximum run-length (number of consecutive 1s or 0s) of the subject protocol is limited (the pattern must be DC-balanced). When the maximum run-length of a protocol is too large, AC-coupling is not possible.

The differential transmitter is paired with a differential receiver - however, while the differential transmitter architecture is relatively standardized there are many different differential receiver architectures in use. A DC-coupled example receiver architecture coupled to the differential transmitter.

One of the advantages of an AC-coupled high-speed link is the control the receiver designer has over the common-mode voltage - the designer can optimize the receive circuit for a specific common mode voltage, because the input signals will not have any DC component. As a result, the jitter requirements of a particular specification can potentially be met with more margin with an AC-coupled receiver than with a DC-coupled receiver.

The result is that the design of a DC-coupled transmitter may be easier than an AC-coupled transmitter for the same set of specifications. Also, the design of an AC-coupled receiver will be easier than the design of a DC-coupled receiver for the same set of specifications.

Reliability/durability

The primary concern for reliability is ESD protection. Since the I/Os for multi-gigabit standards are by definition high data rate, the I/O must have low capacitance. The requirement for low capacitance leads to novel ESD structures to ensure the I/Os are fully protected without introducing the deleterious effects on rise time which result from high capacitance. Such effects include a decrease in supported bandwidth and increases in jitter and power consumption.

Low Speed Communication Interfaces

The most common low speed communications interfaces are I2C, SPI and UART.

The main difference between synchronous interfaces (like the SPI or I2C) and the asynchronous ones (like the UART) is in the way the timing information is passed from transmitter to receiver. Synchronous communication peripherals need a physical line (a wire) to be dedicated to the clock signal, providing synchronization between the two devices

APPENDIX II

References

The electrical hardware system design is complex and requires multidisciplinary expertize. The system quality, durability and cost are dependent on the choices made by the architect.

To familiarize himself on multiple aspects not fully covered in this book, the reader is encouraged to go through following references on circuit design, schematics design, layout design, testing, validation and certification.

http://www.circuitbasics.com/make-custom-pcb/

https://www.pcbcart.com/article/content/pcb-assembly-process.html

https://www.hackster.io/muunbo/how-to-bring-up-a-pcb-cb2a78

https://www.fedevel.com/welldoneblog/2013/10/9-steps-to-bring-up-a-freescale-i-mx6-board-to-life/

https://emcfastpass.com/emc-testing-beginners-guide/emissions/

http://airborn.com.au/method/layout.html

http://www.omnicircuitboards.com/blog/bid/289774/Understanding-PCB-Manufacturing-Multilayer-Assembly

https://www.propertycasualty360.com/2016/04/28/14-things-you-need-to-know-about-commercial-drones/?slreturn=20180816080124

https://www.wired.com/story/guide-drones/

https://wpo-altertechnology.com/drones-product-safety/

© Neeraj Kumar Singh, Porselvan Muthukrishnan, Satyanarayana Sanpini 2019
N. K. Singh et al., *Industrial System Engineering for Drones*,
https://doi.org/10.1007/978-1-4842-3534-8

https://blog.assentcompliance.com/index.php/what-is-product-compliance/

https://www.dekra-product-safety.com/en/solutions/chemical-safety-testing

http://www.tracglobal.com/content/emission-testing

https://www.worldscientific.com/worldscibooks/10.1142/10241

https://top-10-drones.com/blog/choose-motor-propeller-quadcopter/

Epilogue

We set out with a goal of providing good overview and introduction to electrical system design. Reader is taken through fascinating and challenging world of system design, starting from design flow till certification considerations. Drone system example is considered as it encompasses multiple aspects like industrial design, mechanical design, electrical hardware design and real time software designs. Hopefully we succeeded, to a large extent, in providing firm footing, so that reader can explore further on his own.

To develop further expertize and appreciation for the subject matter, reader is encouraged to take up study of few additional embedded system examples like set top box, WiFi routers, IoT systems for home automation, surveillance etc. Studying standard teardown reports is good way to start with. Even more effective approach would be to do a hands on high level design of a small system that addresses a specific need in the real world, however small it may be.

© Neeraj Kumar Singh, Porselvan Muthukrishnan, Satyanarayana Sanpini 2019
N. K. Singh et al., *Industrial System Engineering for Drones*,
https://doi.org/10.1007/978-1-4842-3534-8

Index

© Neeraj Kumar Singh, Porselvan Muthukrishnan, Satyanarayana Sanpini 2019
N. K. Singh et al., *Industrial System Engineering for Drones*,
https://doi.org/10.1007/978-1-4842-3534-8

E

Printed in the United States
By Bookmasters